TRANSFORMING SCHOOL CULTURE

STORIES,

SYMBOLS, VALUES

& The LEADER'S

ROLE

STEPHEN STOLP
STUART C. SMITH

CLEARINGHOUSE ON EDUCATIONAL MANAGEMENT

TRANSFORMING
SCHOOL
CULTURE

STORIES,
SYMBOLS, VALUES
& The LEADER'S
ROLE

STEPHEN STOLP
STUART C. SMITH

CLEARINGHOUSE ON EDUCATIONAL MANAGEMENT
UNIVERSITY OF OREGON
1995

Library of Congress Cataloging-in-Publication Data

Stolp, Stephen Wayne.
    Transforming school culture: stories, symbols, values, and
the leader's role/ Stephen Stolp and Stuart C. Smith ;
foreword by Terrence E. Deal.
       p.   cm.
    Includes bibliographical references.
    ISBN 0-86552-132-8
    1. School management and organization—United States.
2. School environment—United States. 3. School improvement
programs—United States. 4. Educational leadership—United
States. 5. School principals—United States. I. Smith, Stuart
Carl, 1944-   .
II. ERIC Clearinghouse on Educational Management.
III. Title.
LB2805.S748 1995
371.2'00973—dc20   95-19368
                                          CIP

Printed in the United States of America, 1995

Design: LeeAnn August
Type: 10.5/12.5 Palatino
Printer: Thomson-Shore, Dexter, Michigan

ERIC Clearinghouse on Educational Management
  University of Oregon
  1787 Agate Street
  Eugene, OR 97403-5207
  Telephone: (503) 346-5043 Fax: (503) 346-2334
ERIC/CEM Accession Number: EA 026 696

This publication was prepared in part with funding from the Office of Educational Research and Improvement, U.S. Department of Education, under contract no. OERI-RR 93002006. The opinions expressed in this report do not necessarily reflect the positions or policies of the Department of Education. No federal funds were used in the printing of this publication.

The University of Oregon is an equal opportunity, affirmative action institution committed to cultural diversity.

MISSION OF ERIC
AND THE CLEARINGHOUSE

The Educational Resources Information Center (ERIC) is a national information system operated by the U.S. Department of Education. ERIC serves the educational community by disseminating research results and other resource information that can be used in developing more effective educational programs.

The ERIC Clearinghouse on Educational Management, one of several such units in the system, was established at the University of Oregon in 1966. The Clearinghouse and its companion units process research reports and journal articles for announcement in ERIC's index and abstract bulletins.

Research reports are announced in *Resources in Education* (*RIE*), available in many libraries and by subscription from the United States Government Printing Office, Washington, D.C. 20402-9371.

Most of the documents listed in *RIE* can be purchased through the ERIC Document Reproduction Service, operated by Cincinnati Bell Information Systems.

Journal articles are announced in *Current Index to Journals in Education*. *CIJE* is also available in many libraries and can be ordered from Oryx Press, 4041 North Central Avenue at Indian School, Suite 700, Phoenix, Arizona 85012. Semiannual cumulations can be ordered separately.

Besides processing documents and journal articles, the Clearinghouse prepares bibliographies, literature reviews, monographs, and other interpretive research studies on topics in its educational area.

CLEARINGHOUSE
NATIONAL ADVISORY BOARD

Timothy J. Dyer, Executive Director, National Association of Secondary School Principals

Patrick Forsyth, Executive Director, University Council for Educational Administration

Paul Houston, Executive Director, American Association of School Administrators

Joyce G. McCray, Executive Director, Council for American Private Education

Joseph Murphy, Vice-President, Division A, American Educational Research Association

Maggie Rogers, Director, Information Center, Northwest Regional Educational Laboratory

Samuel Sava, Executive Director, National Association of Elementary School Principals

Thomas Shannon, Executive Director, National School Boards Association

Don I. Tharpe, Executive Director, Association of School Business Officials International

Brenda Welburn, Executive Director, National Association of State Boards of Education

ADMINISTRATIVE STAFF

Philip K. Piele, Professor and Director
Stuart C. Smith, Associate Director for Publications

CONTENTS

PREFACE

Today as never before, problems of the outside world encroach on the school environment. Child abuse, gangs, broken families, drugs, violence, and environmental problems all to varying degrees hinder the school's ability to educate students. The challenge for school leaders is to shape and nurture a school culture that can address these growing problems. The school can no longer be seen as just a place for basic instruction. For many students, it serves the function of a home, providing moral direction and a sense of belonging.

The concept of school culture offers school and district leaders a more holistic way to look at the school. By deepening their understanding of culture, school leaders will be better able to influence the values, beliefs, and underlying assumptions held by all members of the school community, with the goal of building an ethos of excellence and caring. Perhaps the most important ability of today's school leader is to be a culture builder, one who instills the values of concern for others, personal and group success, and continuous improvement.

The ERIC Clearinghouse on Educational Management is pleased to publish *Transforming School Culture: Stories, Symbols, Values, and the Leader's Role*, which guides principals, other administrators, and teachers in the process of shaping the culture of their schools. For those who have already begun the process, the book provides insights, examples, and reassurance that their efforts are headed in the right direction.

Stephen Stolp is an assistant professor in the honors college at the University of Oregon. He received his doctoral degree from the University of Oregon in 1993. He has written articles and produced videos on a variety of topics, including educational culture, education for a sense of place, primary socialization, and the use of metaphor in the classroom.

Stuart C. Smith is the Clearinghouse's associate director for publications. He has authored books and articles on faculty collaboration and a variety of issues related to school leadership.

Philip K. Piele
Professor and Director
ERIC Clearinghouse on Educational Management

ACKNOWLEDGMENTS

This book was prepared in cooperation with the Oregon School Study Council, which published an earlier, shorter version in its OSSC Bulletin series (January 1994).

Terrence E. Deal, professor of education at Vanderbilt University, and James W. Keefe, director of research for the National Association of Secondary School Principals, read several drafts and kindly offered many suggestions that added to the book's theoretical and practical value. We especially appreciate the depth and thoroughness of Dr. Keefe's comments and thank him also for sharing with us information on NASSP's Comprehensive Assessment of School Environments program.

Portions of this book will be used as a chapter in *School Leadership: Handbook for Excellence*, third edition, ERIC Clearinghouse on Educational Management, forthcoming.

"School Climate," a chapter in that book's second edition (1989), was written by John Lindelow, Jo Ann Mazzarella, James J. Scott, Thomas I. Ellis, and Stuart C. Smith. The authors of this revision acknowledge the contribution of those earlier writers. Several paragraphs from the 1989 edition have been incorporated into this text.

Meta Bruner performed the keyboarding of successive drafts with her usual skill and good cheer.

Few writers' words have been presented in as appealing a setting, for which we thank LeeAnn August for her cover design and text layout.

FOREWORD

Since time began, humans have recognized the spiritual side of life in human groups. Historically people have struggled to give this elusive, ethereal force a name: mythos, spirit, saga, magic. No matter what name was assigned, people stood in awe of this powerful force because it gave life meaning, passion, and purpose. As both Neitzche and Ibsen observed, life requires supporting illusions and when these illusions wane or burst, the bottom drops out and we lose our way.

In our contemporary world we still struggle to define, create, and maintain the spirit of life in cooperative enterprises. In the early 1980s, businesses refound an old term that anthropologists coined to capture the subterranean forces in human societies—*culture*. Businesses struggled to build or reinforce cultural patterns on the basis of evidence linking a cohesive culture to financial performance. A recent study by Kotter and Hasklett provides ample longitudinal evidence showing that the link between culture and performance is more than imagined.

In education, we called the age-old mysterious force *climate*. Several studies have demonstrated that a positive school climate is associated with academic performance. Other educators called it ethos and again established a linkage between school ethos and academic achievement. Now, along with others, Stephen Stolp and Stuart Smith are introducing culture as an alternative way to capture the powerful spiritual force in schools. While they favor this term as having more value for practitioners than climate, they realize that the blurred boundaries often eclipse efforts to draw clear lines separating the two. They wisely advise practitioners to sort and select whatever ideas they need and use any label they want.

Whatever it is called, the spiritual side of human life is powerful. In today's schools, we desperately need an infusion of passion, purpose, and meaning. Decades of criticism and reform have caused the symbolic tapestry to unravel, robbing students and professionals of faith and life.

Educators' eagerness to reclaim this source of meaning is evident whenever I work in schools. Their responses always tell me when I get to the deeper aspects of culture. It happens when I introduce a different language—history, shared values, heroes and heroines, rituals, ceremony, stories, and the informal network of cultural players (priests and priestesses, story-tellers, gossipers). The language transports people to another level—the world of spirit. My hope is that this book will help educators explore beyond the psychological, structural, and political aspects of educational organizations and discover the power of the symbolic realm to motivate and reenergize both staff and students.

The major contribution Stolp and Smith make is to demonstrate how this symbolic realm can be better understood and shaped through leadership. They provide concrete examples showing the promises and pitfalls of working the existential side of schools. Our (Bolman and Deal) continuing studies of principals time and time again document that the ability to read and respond symbolically is at the heart of effective leadership. Reading this manuscript should help school administrators latch on to an age-old source of wisdom. Thereafter they can help others rediscover the power of symbols in the human experience and as a source of school improvement.

Terrence E. Deal
Professor of Education and Human Development
Vanderbilt Peabody College

PROLOGUE

"Let these describe the undescribable."

Byron

Maybe you are a reader who likes a book to begin with a definition of its topic in the abstract, propositional language academicians are fond of. If that is your expectation as you open this book, you will save time by turning to chapter 1. But if you do, we think you will come away disappointed. Even the best definition cannot adequately convey the breadth and the richness and especially the subtlety of a school's culture. For in the same way that romantic love or the taste of chocolate resists description, abstract words of the type found in most definitions ("values," "symbols," "relationships") somehow fall flat in conveying the meaning of culture.

All is not lost, though. Definitions may fail, but culture comes alive in concrete descriptions of events, social interactions, and classroom behaviors, much like a romantic novel brings us closer to the experience of love. Illustrations, stories, examples, and glimpses into the lives of people who work in schools can help to "describe the undescribable." Thus we begin this book with some simple descriptions of a high school class's ritual, a classroom's architecture, a principal's use of language, and a school's front office. Such language breathes life into the abstract words that necessarily occupy the pages ahead.

A Class Ritual

An assistant principal we'll call Marvin Washington heads a program at a high school for at-risk youth called "Learning to Cope." Most of the students in the program come from broken homes or abusive family situations. They are required to attend group meetings twice a week as a disciplinary action, usually the result of drug use or rude and violent behavior.

The class focuses on a variety of topics and encourages students to talk about their problems at home and school. Sometimes the conversations are angry and emotional. The idea is to let students vent and share their frustrations. Washington hopes the students will gain a sense of community with other students who share similar problems and turn negative energy into positive outcomes.

At the end of each session, regardless of the intensity of emotion in the room, a few minutes are set aside for "high-fives, handshakes, or hugs." The ritual is a consistent part of the program. It requires that students acknowledge each other with a handshake, high-five, or hug. "The intent," says Washington, "is to get kids to realize that they can be angry and still be friends."

By means of this ritual, students physically interact with one another in a way that acknowledges the end of the session and the bond between participants. The perception communicated by the physical act is one of care and concern for one's classmates. But beyond this surface-level understanding, it is also the intent of the ritual to *instill* the values of caring and forgiveness. Washington hopes that when these kids find themselves in other contexts, they will remember the message of a hug: "to forgive and forget." Students express these values as they take lessons beyond the school and apply their experience to other areas of life.

The "Learning to Cope" ritual exemplifies two levels of culture: surface-level experiences and internalized norms and values, which go with us wherever we go.

The Meaning of Classroom Architecture

From behind a large oak desk, William Goldstein looks out at six symmetrical rows. Behind him two chalkboards fill the wall, punctuated in the center with a standard brown-rimmed clock. To his left the 800-square-foot room houses a no-frills high school biology laboratory complete with sinks, black counters, gas, air and water fixtures, a periodic chart of the elements, jars of dead pickled creatures, and a distinct smell of formaldehyde. Brown marble tiles on the floor provide contrast to the white acoustic ceiling panels. A lectern, assignment baskets, and a complete human skeleton surround the front desk. The setting directs attention to Goldstein.

The visible features clearly represent a biology classroom. The architecture, interior design, and furnishings establish the environment. When students or staff enter the room, they realize they have entered a school laboratory, and the desk at the front of the room distinguishes the teacher's place from the students'. These elements are visible and easily recognizable. Students realize they are in a science classroom.

The reality of the classroom, however, goes beyond its physical features. The school also encodes a certain cultural perspective. As Theodore J. Kowalski (1989) states, "The schools we erect today reflect our priorities as a people." They suggest something about the role of education, and their structure reflects a particular cultural orientation.

Goldstein's room represents a microcosm of modern schooling. Straight rows of desks, two chalkboards, a standard clock, textbooks, tile floors, and acoustic ceiling panels reveal more than the classroom's physical environment. They also say something about how our society views education—a more hidden cultural perspective.

The straight rows of desks facing the front of the room are designed to direct students' attention toward the teacher. Hidden in the interior design of the classroom is a cultural value placed on disciplined learning. The hidden value identifies how learn 9ing should take place in Goldstein's classroom. Students should face the front of the room and pay attention to the biology lesson.

The clock denotes the importance of keeping track of time, but it also says something about the school culture: The school places a value on time for the purpose of learning.

We sense a school's culture both in the visible signs that establish an immediate perception and in the norms, values, and beliefs that are implicit in those signs.

A Principal's Style of Communication

School culture offers the practitioner a broader frame of understanding. Relationships are measured by more than just a shared perception. They reflect the history and values of the people and the institution. In this sense, the concept of culture expands an administrator's ability to initiate change in a school setting. Mark Harris of Valley Middle School, one of the principals who was the subject of a case study by Terrence Deal and Kent Peterson, points out that a broader understanding of the school culture allowed him to see how the use of jargon was affecting his daily interactions.

Harris says that the use of "little terms like ITIP and PSAT" really made it difficult to communicate. The acronyms were part of Harris's everyday vocabulary, but often parents and staff failed to understand their meaning. Rather than question Mark about the meaning of such terms, "people just shook their heads like they understood what I was talking about when really they had no idea."

By listening to staff and focusing on relationships, Harris was able to see the down side of what Deal and Peterson call "principal talk"—using a specialized language that only a few understand. So Harris changed not just the acronyms, but the style of his communication. Recognizing and creating a shared language, understood by all, is one way that a cultural perspective can enhance a principal's ability to take a more broad-based approach to change. If he had focused on just the jargon and acronyms, he might have missed the broader-based focus that includes not just the words used in a particular situation, but how the communication process affects relationships.

Mediating change in a school setting requires a sensitivity to shared meaning. Groups organize, coordinate, and take action within a system created by symbolic relationships. "They arrive at certain shared understandings regarding how, when, and where activities are to occur," explain Martin L. Maehr and Leslie J. Fyans, Jr. (1989). The negotiation of these relationships determines the type of change that takes place within a particular culture or institution.

History of a School's Front Office

Walk into the front office of any school and immediately you will sense its personality. The office may appear relaxed or stressful, orderly or disorganized, formal or friendly. The staff may be hurrying around answering phones, typing, and responding to students. These perceptions or impressions are qualities of the immediate environment. Such perceptions, as we explain in chapter 1, constitute the office's *climate.*

To more fully understand an office's culture, one would need to delve into the history of the relationships. For example, one school's front office appears on the surface to operate smoothly and efficiently. A candid talk with the secretary and three clerks, however, reveals that they experience an unhealthy degree of stress because of a system of rules that the principal prescribed two years ago with good intent—to encourage office staff to be productive. The influence of these rules is not easily discernible in the immediate environment. Indeed the principal did not foresee all the consequences of those rules when he instituted them, nor does he perceive them even now. Nevertheless, the stress felt by the office staff and their resentment at having to continue to abide by the principal's rules continue to affect their relationship with him as well as their satisfaction with their jobs.

As this story shows, one aspect of culture is the history of relationships that gives meaning to the present. School culture is the product of a succession of diverse and ever-changing social relationships among those who work and live in the school. In the words of Michael J. Harvey (1991), "The culture of the school emerges from the on-going social interaction of the participants." Does the school's faculty have a history of conflict or collaboration? Why do teachers, who once had a habit of staying at the school until 5:00 p.m., now, with a new principal in the building, quickly head for the parking lot after the last bell has rung? To ask these types of questions—in pursuit of the roots of conflict or a lost work ethic—is to engage in cultural analysis.

We have written this book to help especially principals but also teachers and others to analyze their own school's culture and then to reshape that culture to fit their vision of a healthy school.

INTRODUCTION

School has always been important to me. In junior
high I got straight A-pluses. I was smart. I got A-pluses
up until last semester. If I got an A-minus I would have
a tantrum because I had a high standard for myself. I can't
bear to squeak by with D things. I just can't stand it. You
get criticized, and I don't like criticism of myself. I have
a real high standard.

I started flaking out in school. I would go and just
talk to my friends or write notes or get high and get burnt.
I don't really mind learning, if I'm talking with somebody
and they're telling me something interesting. It's different.
But when you sit in this classroom, it's so, how do you
say, societal. It's just like society. It's sitting in a classroom
with this person teaching you, pointing to the blackboard,
and all these people sitting behind their desks. I don't
know. (Anne Sheffield and Bruce Frankel 1989)

These are the words of Marybeth, a fifteen-
year-old dropout. It would be easy to dismiss Marybeth's
words and classify her as just another outcast that didn't
fit in. We could blame her decision to drop out on a lack
of patience or motivation. We also could blame it on a series
of bad experiences, on her parents, or even on one bad
teacher. The excuses are always easy to imagine. The difficult task is actually to listen to her words.

She is not addressing one specific problem in education.
The scope of Marybeth's concerns are much broader. They
include the structure of schooling, relationships to other
people and institutions, and the value of education. She
reminds educators, surrounded by the minutiae of daily life,
that meeting the needs of students often requires a broader

focus. The expectations of students and staff cannot always be addressed on a case-by-case basis.

The topic of school culture and climate deals with some of these broader issues that concern educational leaders—expressing values and beliefs within the institution, creating a shared vision of schooling, and acknowledging the importance of rituals, ceremonies, and traditions in daily routines. These practices are without a doubt the toughest to implement because there is no single formula. Leaders must exercise both their intellect and intuition and be courageous enough to admit failure when changes are not working.

This book is about recognizing and, if need be, changing a school's culture. Every school has its own unique culture. It is either an ineffective culture, characterized by the absence of vision and cohesiveness, or an effective culture, where staff and students exhibit such qualities as confidence, trust, cooperation, and commitment to do their best. Our goal is to help educators trade in their tired, worn-out, ineffective culture for one that will be a positive force for excellence in their school.

We begin with a discussion in chapter 1 of what *culture* is and how it relates to *climate*. How are these terms similar? How are they different? Chapter 1 provides a framework to help leaders better understand these two terms.

In chapter 2, we establish the importance of culture by reviewing some of the research evidence. Studies both old and new indicate that school culture influences student and teacher motivation, school improvement, leadership effectiveness, and academic achievement.

We probe deeper into the meaning of culture in chapter 3 by examining three levels of organizational culture outlined by Edgar H. Schein (1984): tangible artifacts, values and beliefs, and underlying assumptions. Then in chapter 4 we describe several instruments and qualitative procedures that a leader can use to identify and measure school culture at each of Schein's three levels. By means of these instruments, a leader can seek to better understand the school's existing culture before trying to change it.

In the next three chapters, we offer three perspectives on the process of transforming a school's culture. In chapter 5, we encourage leaders to view the school with a wide angle. Systems thinking helps the culture-builder resist the urge for a quick fix of isolated components of the school and instead encourages discernment of underlying causes and effects.

Vision-building is the focus of chapter 6. The leader does not impose his or her own vision on other members of the school community but rather actively involves them in the process, from conception to implementation.

Finally, in chapter 7, we discuss the leader's role as learner, motivator, and modeler. This chapter also offers a variety of pragmatic strategies and ideas that the leader may find useful in altering a school's culture.

Those who encounter the concept of culture for the first time may find it to be nebulous, vague, impenetrable. But some school leaders already know that the future of students like Marybeth lies in understanding the meaning of this term. Roberto Marquis, principal of Sunset High School in Dallas, Texas, says that "administrators in positions like mine have all but forgotten that the key reason for them being there is to serve the kids, not vice versa." To solve the problem of school dropouts, he says, "You don't have to change anything in the school except the attitude, to an attitude that says kids can do it" (Sheffield and Frankel).

Principal Marquis is exhorting educators to think differently about their students and their environments. Keeping students like Marybeth in school challenges the leader to be more creative and responsive to not only the needs of individual students but the attitudes, values, and beliefs that constitute their school's culture, for those values determine how effective the school will be in motivating Marybeth and others like her to achieve.

1

WHAT ARE SCHOOL CULTURE AND CLIMATE?

Ask any student, teacher, or administrator; indeed, ask anyone who has spent even a short amount of time in different schools: Each has its own distinct "feel" or "personality" that can be recognized soon after entering its doors. At lunch, during class, or in the privacy of the front office, one senses the mood and tenor of a school. Get to know several schools well and you will discover they are as different as the people walking their hallways; at the same time each is as familiar as an old friend.

Some schools are perceived as "good" schools—desirable and perhaps even exciting places to work and learn. Others are perceived as just the opposite—places where one would probably not spend much time were it not for legal or financial compulsions to do so. Still other schools are considered "ordinary" by most observers—not particularly exciting, but not particularly threatening either.

For decades, school researchers and practitioners attempted to capture the "subtle spirit" of a school with the term school *morale*. In the past thirty years or so, this "spirit" has generally been called *school climate*. Both terms have a confusing past, and few educators seem to agree on exactly what the two terms mean. For example, Fritz Steele and Stephen Jenks (1977) defined *school climate* as "what it feels like to spend time in a social system—the weather in that region of social space." Wilbur Brookover and his colleagues (1979) conceived of *climate* as "the composite of norms, expectations, and beliefs which characterize the school social system as perceived by members of the social system."

In more recent years, the term *school culture* has entered the vocabulary of educators. The concept of school culture has emerged from a variety of different sources, but it draws heavily on the concept of organizational culture in the corporate workplace (Terrence Deal 1987 and Terrence Deal and Allan Kennedy 1982). Principles learned from the observation of effectively managed businesses, it has been assumed, can be applied with benefit to the operation of schools.

Origins of the Concept of Culture

The term *culture* has a long history. The meaning of the word has been discussed for many years in a number of different fields, including anthropology, sociology, history, English, and rhetoric. From humanities to the hard sciences, the meaning of the term has inspired conversations and stirred controversy.

Noted anthropologist Clifford Geertz (1973) may have contributed the most to our current understanding of the term. For Geertz, culture represents a "historically transmitted pattern of meaning embodied in symbols." Those symbols include both the written (explicit) and hidden (implicit) messages encoded in language. A school's mission statement may identify some goals in the written text that focus on student achievement. But perhaps not written into the text is the implicit value the school places, or does not place, on academic success. Both the goal (better student achievement) and the underlying value (academic success) are part of school culture.

Some important elements of culture, according to Geertz, are the norms, values, beliefs, traditions, rituals, ceremonies, and myths translated by a particular group of people. Thus, the values expressed in lesson plans and classroom teaching, the way the principal runs staff meetings, and the decorations displayed in hallways are all integral parts of school culture.

Geertz's definition also encompasses many aspects of everyday life. In the school, arguably hall passes, school assemblies, and student hair styles might fit within the boundaries of his definition. For example, the length of students' hair in the late sixties and early seventies reflected not only a hair style but also an implicit political and social perspective. Many students wore their hair long to make a political statement about their relationship to an established authority. At the same time they were affirming their peers who wore their hair in a similar fashion. Along with many other cultural artifacts, length of hair defined a code of meaning that associated people with terms like *hippie* and *beatnik*.

The scope of Geertz's definition is sufficiently broad to include not just verbal or written symbols, but all human symbolic behavior. This behavior includes everything from nonverbal communication (Does a teacher nod and smile when passing a student in the hallway?) to the walls of the school cafeteria (Are they painted in institutional green or decorated with a mural?). The most important aspects of culture are those whose meaning is shared by members of the social system.

Much of the literature on school culture reflects Geertz's interpretation. Terrence Deal and Kent Peterson (1990) refer to culture as "deep patterns of values, beliefs, and traditions that have been formed over the course of [the school's] history." Paul E. Heckman (1993) describes school culture as "the commonly held beliefs of teachers, students, and principals" that guide their actions. Others, like T. W. Maxwell and A. Ross Thomas (1991), suggest that culture is concerned with "those aspects of life that give it meaning."

In summary, we define *school culture* as historically transmitted patterns of meaning that include the norms, values, beliefs, traditions, and myths understood, maybe in varying degrees, by members of the school community.

In practical terms, educators speak of their school's culture when they explain to newcomers "the way we do things around here." Some aspects of culture, however, are not necessarily apparent even to those who work in the school. These are the assumptions that, as Schein (1984) points out, come to be taken for granted and eventually drop out of awareness. But those hidden assumptions continue to shape how people think about their work, relate to their colleagues, define their mission, and derive their sense of identity.

Strong Culture a Prerequisite for Reform

The meaning and importance of culture become clearer when we contrast culture with some other phenomena on the education landscape that typically get more attention.

Site-based management, multiage grouping, inclusive education, and authentic assessment are some of the most popular reforms in the structure, organization, and process of education that are being instituted in schools today. Educators and policy-makers have also sought, at various times, to improve the performance of schools through merit pay, performance-based budgeting, differentiated staffing, better testing and accountability systems, and a host of other programs and structures that have been implemented in classrooms, schools, districts, and even entire states.

"What we have learned from a long history of structural change is that it does not work!" exclaim William G. Cunningham and Donn W. Gresso (1993). Educators, often on the advice of innovative scholars, have been tinkering with the structure and organization of schools for decades with the assumption that an appropriate structure will produce an effective work culture. Cunningham and Gresso say the truth is just the opposite: "Structure should not be used to change organizational performance and effectiveness. It should be vice versa—focus on the culture of excellence and the structures will evolve to support that culture."

In a recent study of factors that contribute to the development of professional community in schools, Karen Seashore Louis, Helen M. Marks, and Sharon Kruse (1994) found evidence in support of

> the argument that the structural elements of "restructuring" have received excessive emphasis in many reform proposals, while the need to improve the culture, climate and interpersonal relationships in schools have received too little attention. While it may be easier to imagine how to restructure schools rather than to change their culture, the latter is the key to successful reform.

Why does culture exert such a powerful influence on a school's effectiveness? Because the culture tells people in the school what is truly important and how they are to act. As Bruce A. Lane (1992) says, "The power of the school culture model lies in its recognition that movement of schools toward greater effectiveness must begin with attention to the subtle, habitual regularities of behavior that comprise the culture of the school." If, for example, a principal wishes to bring about more collegiality in a school that has had a culture of teacher isolation, a first step might be to initiate some rituals of transition to help teachers cope with the loss of their independence and predictable routines (Lane, Deal 1987).

Leaders who are cognizant of the cultural realm know that there is yet another crucial way in which culture determines effectiveness. People commit their energy only to what they believe in, what captures their enthusiasm and imagination. The sad reality is that in schools lacking a culture of excellence, people labor without inspiration. As Cunningham and Gresso state, "There is a lack of excitement in the symbols, traditions, stories and sagas of the institutions. The culture serves as a self-perpetuating counterforce to effectiveness."

Some of the structural innovations referred to above have a lot of potential to improve schools, but only when supported by an effective culture. The challenge for leaders is to develop a consensus around values that constitute an effective culture, such as high expectations, commitment, mutual respect, confidence, continuous improvement, experimentation and risk-taking, and an insistence that students will learn. If individuals buy in to these beliefs, values, and behaviors, the school and all its members will succeed. In later chapters we look at some steps leaders can take to build such a culture.

Relationship Between Culture and Climate

If culture plays such a pervasive and vital role in the life of the school, how does the concept of climate fit in? We regard climate as a narrower concept than culture. *Climate* is the term typically used to describe people's shared perceptions of the organization or work unit, whereas *culture*, as we have seen, embraces not only how people feel about their organization, but the assumptions, values, and beliefs that give the organization its identity and specify its standards for behavior. When discussing climate, the focus is on the impressions, feelings, and expectations held by members of the school organization. These perceptions are aroused by the organization's structure and setting, as well as by the social interactions among those who work and learn there.

James Keefe (1993) notes that climate may in practice be understood as one measure of culture. He further differentiates between *climate* (perceptions of culture that are shared by members of an organization) and *satisfaction* (the view of aspects of the organization's culture held by each individual).

A teacher once suggested, "It's easier to feel a part of culture than climate. Climate is something that we are told surrounds us, not necessarily something that is an integral part of us. Culture we take with us wherever we go." These words capture an important contrast. Culture, because it embraces not only the immediate environment but also what people believe and value, provides a more inclusive framework. The interactions between humans and their climate are a necessary part of culture, but human expressions of culture are not always part of the climate. This is an important distinction in defining the essential characteristics of these two concepts.

Culture: An Expanded Vision

Culture and climate can be represented by two circles, as depicted in figure 1. Culture includes climate, but climate does not encompass all aspects of culture. This is one reason that understanding culture is so critical for the practitioner. Examples of how two imaginary high school principals sought to improve their faculty's effectiveness illustrate the expanded vision culture offers the practitioner.

At Claremont High School, Principal Jennifer Brown wanted to build a collaborative work environment for teachers. To lay groundwork for the collaborative process, Principal Brown offered a retreat for faculty members in which they shared their previous experiences of working with colleagues, discussed the benefits and costs of collaboration, and wrote a statement of the values and beliefs that would guide them as a learning community. She then had the teachers form work teams to plan the instructional activities on which they would collaborate during the coming school year.

Across town at Jackson High School, Principal Jerome Thomas also wanted to foster faculty collaboration. As a first

FIGURE 1

Dimensions for Distinguishing Between Culture and Climate

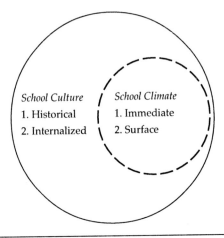

School Culture
1. Historical
2. Internalized

School Climate
1. Immediate
2. Surface

step, he polled the faculty to find out its concerns about collaboration. When the teachers overwhelmingly said there was no time in their workday for meeting with their colleagues, Principal Thomas decided the best strategy was to free teachers from class time one hour each week so they would have more time to meet together for collegial planning and decision-making.

These two principals had a common goal, but Principal Thomas's strategy focused more on climate. He changed the immediate environment by giving teachers more time to plan. Principal Brown chose a broader cultural approach by focusing on the values and beliefs of teachers. She wasn't content to elicit the opinions of teachers and, in response, implement a structural change; rather, she stimulated teachers to think about their philosophy of what a faculty ought to be. Each principal's strategy can be effective, but as the circles in figure 1 illustrate, only the framework of culture includes both principals' strategies. Because the cultural perspective allows for more indepth analysis over time, it expands an administrator's framework of understanding and ability to effect change.

By way of summary, we can distinguish between culture and climate along the two dimensions listed in figure 1.

Historical versus Immediate: Culture is a product of the history of relationships in a school, whereas climate is defined by how people perceive those relationships in the present. (This is not to suggest people's perceptions readily change from day to day; in fact, school climate, like culture, is relatively stable.)

Internalized versus Surface: Culture has to do with the values and assumptions underlying behavior, whereas climate is based on people's perceptions of the behavior itself. The values underlying spoken words or the design of a school may not be easily detected, whereas climate is the perception that people share about what is immediately visible.

Although these dimensions are conceptually helpful, it is not possible to mark the boundaries between school culture and climate with precision. As the broken circle dividing culture and climate in the figure suggests, the categories are not meant to be absolute or rigid. These dimensions denote some unique qualities of climate and culture while still recognizing their inseparable relationship. But the lines are never definitive; the boundaries are represented not by fine lines, but by transitional shades of gray. Indeed, we must remember that climate emerges from people's shared perception of culture.

Deal (1993) states: "Formal definitions, though verifiable and rigorous, often fail to capture the robustness of a concept as experienced by those that know it first hand." In other words, most practitioners don't care what you call it as long as it works. As the principal of a Portland, Oregon, middle school put it, "At a certain point I just have to deal with reality."

Limitations on the Term 'Culture'

We have seen that the concept of school culture is particularly valuable to school leaders who wish to change their organizations, but along with this benefit the concept also carries some liabilities. The impossibility of completely separating culture from its counterpart term is only one of the practical issues that arise when the concept of culture is applied to schools. Let's look at a few others.

Culture is a broad term that enjoys usage in several disciplines. Each field uses the term to explain a variety of different ideas and phenomena. At some point the broad-scale use of *culture* fails to give meaning to every application. The framework can become so broad as to be meaningless. Principals may talk about anything as a cultural artifact. This lack of focus could leave an administrator confused about which aspects of culture to feature.

Part of the problem stems from the difficulty of characterizing culture in practical, concrete terms. Social scientists have long failed to operationalize or accurately measure culture. This inability to "calculate culture" may reflect the subjective nature of feelings, beliefs, values, traditions, and other symbolic expressions. Because of its subjectivity, culture cannot be easily computed, calculated, or constricted by scientific analysis. Perhaps the best appraisals of culture are those that employ a variety of perspectives with an eye toward description. The ideal characterization may be one that looks toward an understanding of systemic patterns and relationships. In this sense culture provides a template for evaluating and assessing the role of the leader in a school setting.

Building a Shared Understanding

The broad meaning of culture limits the usefulness of this term, but the lack of a specific definition reveals only part of the problem. Teachers and administrators have become comfortable with the term *climate*, which has become an integral part of the ongoing conversation in everyday school life. As Maxwell and Thomas point out, "Teachers use it because they understand it and it gives them explanatory power." For this reason, Richard J. Bates (1987) and D. S. Finlayson (1987) warn against manipulating teachers to discard the term, which may represent a point at which teachers have developed a shared understanding. Acknowledgment of this shared meaning is certainly an important consideration to those who want to introduce *culture* to educators' vocabulary.

At the very least, leaders can expand this shared meaning without necessarily using new terminology. While avoiding use of the *word* culture, they can draw attention to some of its more valuable *concepts*: the values, beliefs, and assumptions that shape teachers' and administrators' vision of an excellent education. School leaders who ignore efforts to differentiate between culture and climate would not be in bad company, because even many scholars do exactly that. Although the imprecision may be awkward, we would gladly subordinate our preference for precise language to anything that makes it easier for educators to build strong school cultures.

Creative Use of Both Terms

Notwithstanding its limitations, the benefits of using culture as a way to understand broad-based change in the school are compelling. The concept of culture provides for a deeper understanding of symbolic systems, historical contexts, and social relationships. The point is not to rid ourselves of the term *climate*, but rather to find some shared understanding that allows for the creative use of both terms. So as we continue our discussion of culture and climate, we will remember the importance of each. *Climate* defines people's shared perceptions of an environment, and *culture* captures a deeper meaning embedded in the history of that environment.

In the chapters ahead, you will encounter both terms, but not necessarily in the way we have defined them. This is because when citing other authors, we have retained their terminology. Writers seem to favor *climate* even when, by our definition, they really mean *culture*. You will have to discern from the context whether the researchers and other writers we cite are referring to the broader concept of values, beliefs, and assumptions or the narrower realm of perceptions.

We have tried, however, not to focus on terminology, but the power of the symbolic realm to make a real difference in the productivity of educational organizations.

In chapter 2, attention turns to the effects of a healthy culture and climate as studied by researchers. Is the effort to improve culture and climate worthwhile? This question is worth pursuing.

2

THE IMPORTANCE OF SCHOOL CULTURE: EVIDENCE FROM THE RESEARCH

"The most important foundational element is the culture of the school."

Allan A. Glatthorn (1992)

Does it really matter whether a school has a "healthy" culture? Is it worth taking the trouble to try to improve culture? What would be the rewards of such an undertaking?

Certainly the satisfaction and morale of students and staff are higher in schools with healthy cultures than in schools with unhealthy ones. Indeed, many instruments designed to measure school culture and climate do so indirectly by measuring satisfaction with the school. But is there any hard evidence that culture influences the final outcomes of education—how much and how well children learn? A large body of research on the characteristics of effective schools briefly reviewed in this chapter indicates that it does.

Researchers have accumulated some compelling evidence in support of the proposition that deliberate changes in a school's culture and climate* can make the school a place in which teachers feel positive about their work and students are motivated to learn. A positive school culture is associated with higher student motivation and achievement, increased teacher collaboration, and improved attitudes among teachers toward their jobs. In this chapter, we review a number of studies that emphasize the importance of culture

---

* This brief review of research includes some studies that focused on school climate and some that assessed school culture. Astute readers will note that in most cases these two terms refer to approximately the same phenomena. That is because we have retained the authors' terminology rather than attempted to force a distinction between the terms along the lines expressed in chapter 1. Older studies used the term *climate* almost exclusively, whereas *culture* has grown in popularity in recent years.

in areas such as student and teacher motivation, academic achievement, and creating safe and collaborative learning environments.

Landmark Studies

Two of the best known studies are those conducted in the 1970s by Wilbur Brookover and colleagues (1979) and by Michael Rutter and colleagues (1979). Despite their age, these studies still provide some important insights.

Brookover's team studied 91 elementary schools chosen at random from the 2,200 elementary schools in Michigan with fourth- and fifth-grade students. Altogether, 11,466 students, 453 teachers, and 91 principals participated in the study.

From school records and from questionnaires administered to the students, teachers, and principals, the researchers obtained data on "inputs" into the school system. Data included both demographic variables (such as the socioeconomic status and racial composition of a school's students) and school climate variables (such as students', teachers', and principals' perceptions of their abilities to function successfully within the school). In addition to measuring such "inputs" into the schools, the study measured certain "outcome variables": the achievement scores of the fourth-grade students on state-administered math and reading tests, measures of the students' self-concepts of academic ability, and measures of students' sense of "self-reliance."

Although a relationship existed between school climate and the economic and racial composition of the student bodies, the authors demonstrated that their climate variables had a stronger influence on achievement than did the racial and economic ones. "Although it is not sufficient proof," they concluded, "these analyses suggest that school climate rather than family background as reflected in student body composition has the more direct impact on achievement."

In another landmark study, a team of researchers led by Michael Rutter followed the progress of a group of children from London's inner city through the first three years after they entered secondary school, comparing behavior and performance at the beginning of the period to those at the end.

After correcting for such variables as student socioeconomic status and family background, the researchers still found that students "were more likely to show good behavior and good scholastic attainments if they attended some schools than if they attended others."

Rutter and colleagues suggested that differences in school climate contributed to these differences in student performance. They found that the combined effect on school outcomes of the school process variables they measured was much stronger than the effect of any individual process variable.

> This suggests that the *cumulative* effect of these various social factors was considerably greater than the effect of any of the individual factors on their own. The implication is that the individual actions or measures may combine to create a particular *ethos*, or set of values, attitudes and behaviours which will become characteristic of the school as a whole.

NASSP's Comprehensive Assessment of School Environments

In 1982, the National Association of Secondary School Principals created a task force to investigate the literature on school climate. After considerable review, the committee decided new instruments were needed to assess climate and the total school environment. The result was the Comprehensive Assessment of School Environments—Information System Management. According to Eugene R. Howard and James W. Keefe (1991), the CASE-IMS model consists of variables designed to assess many aspects of the school environment, from student achievement and motivation to principal leadership and teacher satisfaction.

The variables that form the foundation for the CASE model were identified in a series of pilot studies that began in 1985 and a nationwide normative study in 1988. The latter study involved a random sample of 364 middle schools and high schools in 36 states and Canada, including urban, suburban, exurban, and rural areas. The sample of 364 principals, 14,721 teachers, and 24,874 students were asked to respond to CASE-IMS surveys.

Principals provided standardized achievement test data for every grade in their schools in the subjects of reading comprehension, math, and science. In addition, they were asked about attitudes within the school toward change and school improvement, the availability of resources, the performance of the administrative team, their degree of autonomy from the central office in making decisions, and other matters. Teachers answered questions about school goals, school climate, school commitment, participation in decision-making, degrees of autonomy, and job satisfaction. Students responded to questions about school climate, self-efficacy, satisfaction with teachers, and overall satisfaction. Responses from both teachers and students were aggregated to the school level.

Upon analyzing the data, the researchers identified thirty-four variables that "seemed useful in understanding the effectiveness and efficiency of schools and in making recommendations for interventions." The task force concluded, "What schools and the people in them *do* and *believe* makes a difference in student outcomes." The authors suggest that teacher climate "is related to the achievement variables, disciplinary actions, and percentage of students passing even when the effects of socioeconomic status (as represented by the percent of free lunch participants) are held constant." The NASSP study emphasizes the importance of maintaining a healthy school climate.

A study summarized in the next section demonstrates the importance of school culture in efforts to reform schools.

Culture and School Reform

Successful school reform requires commitment from all who participate in the process of education. Teachers are especially critical to the process of reform, because they control the quality, mood, and tempo of daily instruction. Less-than-cooperative teachers make systemic change nearly impossible.

A research project by Leithwood, Jantzi, and Fernandez (1994) addressed some of the important variables that influence the success of school reform. Specifically their research evaluated the relationship between school culture and teacher commitment to change.

For their study, the researchers surveyed staff members in 9 secondary schools about "perceptions of conditions affecting their school improvement efforts." The 9 schools were located in an urban school district consisting of more than 140 schools. The total school population included 26,000 students and 1,700 teachers. District-level personnel nominated the 9 schools chosen for the study based on significant engagement in school-improvement efforts. A total of 168 teachers in the 9 schools responded to the questionnaire, and virtually all respondents (91 percent) were involved in school-improvement efforts.

Teacher perceptions about conditions for school improvement were measured in three areas: personal goals, belief in the school's commitment to change efforts, and belief in the ability or capacity of the school to meet those change efforts. These variables were analyzed in relation to the school's culture, policies, programs, resources, and other conditions. The variables were also measured in relation to leadership styles such as vision-creating, modeling, expectations, consensus-building, and intellectual stimulation.

The first level of results reported by the researchers focused on the importance of certain leadership qualities. Leadership practices that had the greatest influence on teacher commitment to change were creating vision and building consensus around goals. These practices had a significant influence on teachers' motivation for change. In addition, teachers' belief in the school's commitment to change and capacity for change increased dramatically when leaders had a strong vision and willingness to work toward change together with teachers and staff.

The second level of results related to school restructuring and culture building. According to Leithwood, Jantzi, and Fernandez, "Conditions in the school, as teachers interpret them, have the strongest direct effects on teachers' commitment to change." "This suggests," the researchers say, "the need for school leaders, first of all, to attend consciously to the content, strength, and form of their school's culture." School culture in this study was the most significant factor in determining the success of school restructuring. The authors conclude that strategies for building school culture are crucial for any successful school reform and restructuring effort.

The researchers suggest several strategies that leaders might consider on the road to school restructuring. These include "selecting staff whose values reflect those considered important to the school, telling stories that illustrate shared values, using symbols and rituals to express cultural values, and sharing power and responsibility with others."

Professional Community

If the goal of school reform is to develop schools in which teachers actively take responsibility for student learning, what is the best way to attain this goal? Is the answer better professional development to upgrade teachers' skills and knowledge? This may not be a bad idea, say three researchers at the Center on Organization and Restructuring of Schools, "but our data suggest that professional development is less important in producing professional community—and, therefore, responsibility for student learning—than changing the climate and culture of the school."

An element that is missing in the systemic reform and teacher professionalization movements, state Karen Seashore Louis, Helen M. Marks, and Sharon Kruse (1994), is "the development of schools as healthy, professionally sustaining environments in which teachers are encouraged to do their best job."

The researchers analyzed data collected between 1991 and 1994 in the center's School Restructuring Study. Teams of researchers visited eight elementary, eight middle, and eight high schools across the nation that had made substantial progress in restructuring. In addition, 910 teachers completed questionnaires on their instructional practices, their schools' culture, and other aspects of their professional backgrounds and activities.

In the first stage of their analysis, Louis and her colleagues sought to determine whether the structural characteristics of schools and their human and social resources influence the development of professional community among teachers. In the second stage, they investigated the effect of this professional community on teachers' responsibility for student learning.

Schoolwide *professional community*, as the researchers conceive it, is measured by six components: "shared sense of purpose, collaborative activity, collective responsibility, collective focus on student learning, deprivatized practice, and reflective dialogue." In turn, they regard *teacher responsibility for student learning* as a set of beliefs and attitudes concerning students' capability to learn and teachers' confidence that they can make a difference in students' lives.

Louis and her colleagues found that changes in two aspects of the school's structure—providing more time for teachers to collaborate and empowering them to make key decisions about school policy—do contribute to professional community. But more critical than structure are several elements related to the school's human and social conditions: the extent to which teachers feel supported by the school administration; the respect they receive from their colleagues, administrators, and others in the school community; and their openness to innovation. These conditions were more strongly related to professional community than were the structural factors.

Elementary schools as a group had stronger professional communities than did middle schools and high schools, but one high school in the innercity of a large metropolitan area scored very high in community. A school of choice that serves 450 poor students and adheres to principles of the Coalition of Essential Schools, it emphasizes reinforcing "habits of the mind" and is organized into interdisciplinary teams. "Teachers are constantly in-and-out of each other' classrooms, and indicate that they have a strong sense of accountability to each other for the quality of their performance," Louis and her colleagues say.

The high schools that had weaker professional communities were "less far along in creating a consensus about goals and a language of reform," they write. Reform proposals met with opposition. Because of their size and organization in departments, high schools understandably face more obstacles than elementary schools in building schoolwide community.

The researchers concluded that "professional community clearly enhances teachers' sense of responsibility for student learning." Therefore, efforts to encourage teachers to come to consensus on schoolwide goals, to collaborate on curriculum articulation, and to define the standards for which they will hold one another accountable have great value. Activities like these will help to increase teachers' sense of mastery and their influence on student learning—vital ingredients for a school culture of excellence.

Student Motivation

Several studies suggest that the ability to recognize and alter cultural patterns within the school can provide valuable outcomes. Leslie J. Fyans, Jr. and Martin L. Maehr (1990) offer one such example. Their research suggests that school culture plays an important role in determining student motivation and achievement. The results are particularly applicable for a variety of different ethnic groups.

Fyans and Maehr distributed 16,310 questionnaires to fourth-, sixth-, eighth-, and tenth-grade students from 820 different schools in the Illinois public school system. The students represented a diverse ethnic population from both rural and urban areas.

These two researchers assessed five dimensions of school culture: emphasis on excellence and pursuit of academic challenges; emphasis on interpersonal competition and socially comparative achievement; emphasis on social recognition for achievement; perceived sense of community; and perception that the school stresses certain purposes and goals. These five areas were measured against a scale designed to assess student motivation.

Students in the study were given the questionnaire and asked to compare varying degrees of motivation in relation to the five dimensions of school culture. The students answered questions such as "How important is it for you to do well on a test?", "When I perform well on an assignment in school, it is because...", and "Does this school give recognition for good performance?" Students' answers to these questions helped the researchers to characterize the relationship between school culture and student motivation.

Fyans and Maehr concluded, "Clearly, these studies present strong preliminary evidence that the perceived culture of the school relates to motivation and ultimately school achievement." Although "psychological environments" play different roles, school culture was found to be "important for the motivation of children of different ethnic backgrounds." These results were consistent with those of earlier studies by Fyans and Maehr that also identified a relationship between school culture and academic achievement.

Student Achievement

The findings of two other studies also support the changing of academic culture to improve student achievement. A study by Jerry L. Thacker and William D. McInerney (1992) came about in response to slipping student test scores in the Metropolitan School District of Lawrence Township, Indiana. Lower than expected test scores on the Indiana Statewide Test of Educational Progress endangered accreditation at several schools.

As a result, school staff, parents, community members, and students joined together to create a massive improvement project that focused on school culture. The school-improvement model included:

- a mission statement
- goals based on outcomes for all students
- curriculum alignment corresponding with those goals
- staff development
- building-level decision-making
- input from school board members, school principals, teachers, other school employees, pupils, parents and students attending school, and other residents

The school-improvement plan was outcome oriented and addressed what the people involved felt were the essential changes necessary to make school culture more productive. Their goals were expressed clearly in the superintendent and community board's mission statement:

- All children can and will learn the Indiana proficiencies.
- All schools will show improvement in language arts and mathematics achievement test scores.
- Parents will be involved in and supportive of the efforts to have their children master the Indiana

proficiencies.

Principals and other administrators played a key role in translating the mission statement into a shared vision at the school level. Under the new vision, student-readiness activities were favored over remediation; "learning well" was favored over "selecting and sorting" students; and students in need of remediation, instead of relying on summer school, were given extended opportunities to finish school work.

The results were encouraging. The number of students who failed the Indiana statewide test dropped at the first-grade level by over 10 percent, second-grade by 5 percent, and third-grade by 5 percent. Because of the significant improvement, every elementary school received state award monies.

Thacker and McInerney conclude that the focus on school culture—particularly the implementation of a shared vision—promoted many of these changes.

The recent work of Samuel E. Krug (1992) also supports the relationship between school climate and student achievement. Krug describes climate as "the attitudinal infrastructure" of a school. Out of 81 Chicago-area schools, he selected 1,523 teachers and approximately 40,000 students to participate in the study.

A variety of instruments were used to assess instructional leadership and school climate. Principals completed the Instructional Leadership Inventory and the School Administrator Assessment Survey; teachers filled out the Instructional Climate Inventory (Form T); and students completed either the Instructional Climate Inventory (Form S) or the Illinois Goal Assessment Program.

After evaluating all the data, Krug found a significant correlation between the instructional climate and student-achievement scores. He also reported a positive correlation between instructional leadership and the instructional climate.

Leadership and Organizational Culture

The research of Marshall and Molly G. Sashkin (1990) supports an "interrelationship" between leadership and organizational culture. These two researchers assessed leadership and culture in twelve different schools in one district. They collected data from principals, vocational education supervisors, teachers, and students.

Using three instruments, the Leader Behavior Questionnaire (LBQ), the School Culture Assessment Questionnaire (SCAQ), and "Frames of Reference," Sashkin and Sashkin measured leadership characteristics such as self-efficacy and the leader's impact on organizational culture in relation to group factors like attaining goals, working together as a team, and sharing values and beliefs. They first measured leadership behaviors with the LBQ and then correlated the findings with the SCAQ and "Frames of Reference."

The results point to "a strong web of relationships . . . among leadership variables and organizational culture." The variables with the highest correlation included "a relationship between visionary leadership behavior and teamwork, between time-span and use of symbols, between culture building and adaptation, and between culture building and strength of shared values and beliefs." According to the Sashkins, all these relationships were statistically significant.

In a similar study at the district level, J. Endeman (1990) also found a relationship between visionary leadership and district culture.

Strong versus Weak Cultures

Yin Cheong Cheng (1993) profiled effective and ineffective organizational cultures in thirty-two schools, sixteen with "strong culture" and the other half with "weak culture." The distinction between strong and weak was decided on the basis of a variety of organizational characteristics. Strength of organizational ideology, participation, intimacy, charismatic leadership style, and authority hierarchy represent just a few of the limiting variables.

After determining the variables that correlate with weak and strong cultures, Cheng compared the schools in the areas of organizational structure, teacher job attitude, and school effectiveness. "Strong culture," Cheng concluded, "is associated with positive organizational characteristics, teachers' job attitudes, and students' academic outcomes." That is, teachers who enjoy their jobs and students who do well academically are more likely to be found in strong school cultures than in weak ones.

Terrence Deal and Kent Peterson, in *The Principal's Role in Shaping School Culture* (1990), offer five case studies, each presenting different reasons why school culture is important. For example, Frances Hedges of Orchard Park Elementary School in San Francisco emphasizes culture as a way to build a sense of community. Hank Cotton of Cherry Creek High School in Denver features a cultural approach to solving problems such as absenteeism, drug use, and violence. All five case studies contain instances of both success and failure, but on balance Deal and Peterson say their evidence suggests that culture is a critical element in the process of school reform.

> We believe that the more principals understand about school culture and their roles in shaping it, the better equipped they will be to avoid the common pitfalls of change and reform. Culture involves all dimensions of life in schools. It determines individual needs and outlooks, shapes formal structures, defines the distribution of power, and establishes the means by which conflicts are dealt with. Understanding the specific culture of a school helps principals make external reforms locally meaningful. (Deal and Peterson)

Not only is culture a determinant of the process of change, but a healthy culture can also support safe and collaborative learning environments.

Safe and Unsafe Schools

Audrey James Schwartz (1990) surveyed and interviewed students and teachers from nineteen high schools in the Los Angeles area. The surveys and interviews focused on the relationship between students and teachers in different types of schools. Schwartz looked at two distinct settings: schools defined as most safe with least gang activity and those considered least safe with most gang activity. Based on interviews with teachers and students, the schools were coded as favorable and unfavorable school contexts.

Schwartz concluded that "many teachers in unfavorable school contexts lack strong commitment to their school social system." Her findings point to a significant correlation between poor school culture and inhibited teacher collaboration. In her words, "Unfavorable school contexts reinforce the attributes of traditional teacher culture that inhibit teacher collaboration." So strong are the results that Schwartz urges school leaders to closely examine school culture before proceeding with any reform or restructuring plans.

These and other studies offer a variety of perspectives for understanding the complex nature of school culture. They tell us why school culture is important—for student and teacher motivation, teacher collaboration, school reform, problem solving, community building, and student achievement.

Lessons of Experience

Researchers help illuminate part of the mosaic, but some of the best understanding comes from personal experience. Those who spend time in the classrooms, front offices, hallways, lunch rooms, and gymnasiums, and pay attention to how relationships change over time, know the importance of school culture. Most any principal or teacher who instructs students, talks to parents, attends meetings, walks the school grounds, or monitors the lunch room will acknowledge the influence of school culture.

Practitioners derive valuable lessons from personal experience. The meaningful examples are lived as part of everyday life or shared in personal accounts. As middle-school Principal Jane Arkes reminds the practitioner, "Some things just take time and experience." To understand the importance of school culture, a person needs only to consider the relationships around them. These are the critical links between the practitioner and his or her cultural environment.

THREE LEVELS OF CULTURE

"**W**hat do you lose when you stand up?" A first- grader shouted across four rows of monkey bars to his friend swinging upside down by his legs. "Your stomach!" the joke teller answered before his friend had a chance to reply. The riddle initiated a hysterical fit of laughter from both children. Neither seemed particularly concerned that the answer was incorrect. "You lose your lap not your stomach," advised an older brother, but that didn't stop the children from repeating the same joke several times and roaring in laughter again and again.

Unlike the brother, the two first-graders shared a similar understanding. Between them, the riddle provided an agreed-upon code of meaning. The riddle was still funny even without the "correct" answer. For the two younger kids, losing a stomach *was* the "correct" answer. What the older boy—the "outsider"—considerd a nonsensical exchange had a shared humorous meaning for the two younger children.

We recognize change in school culture and climate in much the same way that the two first-graders understand their private riddle. We develop a shared language. Like the first-graders' humorous exchange, culture and climate grow out of shared meanings. Interactions in the classrooms, hallways, or front offices become part of how teachers, students, parents, and administrators understand their school setting. The language is often foreign to an outsider. As was the case with the two youngsters, the participants in school contexts may be the only ones who truly understand it.

The school develops a unique language of sorts. Teachers discuss inservice workshops, referrals, bus duty, and progress reports, while principals and other staff consider discipline policies, curriculum guides, scheduling, and PTA requests. Even the school building represents part of the symbolic message with its lockers, posters, bells, and chalkboards. These and many other subtle messages fill the busy spaces of school life.

To an outsider, the meaning of the language of schools often seems hidden, like the lap that "goes away" when we stand. That is because the school culture is expressed in different levels of abstraction. Schein (1984) suggests organizational culture exists at three levels: "the artifacts level, the values and beliefs level, and the underlying assumptions level."

Schein's model offers insight into the complicated meaning of culture by uncovering different levels of abstraction. His work is representative of a variety of other studies that describe culture as a system of relationships and shared meanings. The model provides a valuable template. It allows for description of the different levels of culture in an explanatory but not exclusive manner.

Tangible Artifacts

The "artifacts level," the most visible of the three, is perhaps the level most closely associated with what we think of as school climate—how people perceive the school. A school's artifacts are those daily rituals, ceremonies, and icons that are most conspicuous to the casual observer. Students' math papers, roll call in class, the bell for first period, and the smell of a long hallway represent elements of the artifacts level of culture.

The initial "feel" of the school emanates from this tangible level of experience. Thus, people who appear at the school for the first time are most likely to recognize this level of culture. They may experience it as a mood or feeling, a certain style, or a physical presence. Consider two different first impressions as illustrated in Jonathan Kozol's *Savage Inequalities* (1991):

Case One

In order to find Public School 261 in District 10, a visitor is told to look for a mortician's office. The funeral home, which faces Jerome Avenue in the North Bronx, is easy to identify by its green awning. The school is next door, in a former roller-skating rink. No sign identifies the building as a school. A metal awning frame without an awning supports a flagpole, but there is no flag.

In the street in front of the school there is an elevated public transit line. Heavy traffic fills the street. The existence of the school is virtually concealed within this crowded city block.

In a vestibule between the outer and inner glass doors of the school there is a sign with these words: "All children are capable of learning."

Beyond the inner doors a guard is seated. The lobby is long and narrow. The ceiling is low. There are no windows. All the teachers that I see at first are middle-aged white women. The principal, who is also a white woman, tells me that the school's "capacity" is 900 but that there are 1,300 children here. The size of classes for fifth and sixth grade children in New York, she says, is "capped" at 32, but she says that class size in the school goes "up to 34.". . . Lack of space, she says, prevents the school from operating a pre-kindergarten program.

I ask the principal where her children go to school. "They are enrolled in private school," she says.

Case Two

The train ride from Grand Central Station to suburban Rye, New York, takes 35 to 40 minutes. The high school is a short ride from the station. Built of handsome gray stone and set in a landscaped campus, it resembles a New England prep school. On a day in early June of 1990, I enter the school and am directed by a student to the office.

The principal, a relaxed, unhurried man who, unlike many urban principals, seems gratified to have me visit in his school, takes me in to see the auditorium, which, he says, was recently restored with private charitable funds ($400,000) raised by parents. The crenelated ceiling, which is white and spotless, and the polished dark-wood paneling contrast with the collapsing structure of the auditorium at Morris High. The principal strikes his fist against a balcony: "They made this place extremely solid." Through a window, one can see the spreading branches of a beech tree in the central courtyard of the school.

In a student lounge, a dozen seniors are relaxing on a carpeted floor that is constructed with a number of tiers so that, as the principal explains, "they can stretch out and be comfortable while reading."

These two cases illustrate two distinctly different expressions of school culture at the artifacts level. Kozol describes those elements of culture that make us most readily aware of its existence. It is not difficult to notice the difference between the educational settings in these two New York schools. If we want to trace the complex pattern of school culture, we should begin at the artifacts level, but identification of culture at this level only scratches the surface of understanding. We only get a glimpse of the complete picture. The second level of culture provides deeper analysis into the values and beliefs that guide a community or school.

Values and Beliefs

The "values and beliefs level," according to Schein, defines the basic organizational character of the school. As the National LEADership Network Study Group on Restructuring Schools suggests, "Through shared values and beliefs, members of the organization develop a sense of direction that guides their day-to-day behavior" (Joan Burnham and Shirley Hord 1993). Values are enacted as part of the daily school routine. If the school has designated respect as an important value, people are expected to treat others with consideration and concern.

Likewise, teachers, principals, and other staff express certain beliefs about the value of education. Practitioners bring with them a particular set of principles that reflect the very nature of education at the school. For example, a teacher may believe in the value of experiential learning. This belief, then, becomes an expression of culture as reflected in her actions.

Values and beliefs are not always explicit, however. They are often a reflection of experience. Our verbal and written symbols encode what we value and believe, and so do the hidden or implicit dimensions of our language. A sign in a school's front office says, "A clean desk is a sign of a sick mind." The sign is not intended to be taken literally. Not all people who have clean desks are mentally ill; rather, the sign speaks to a cultural norm. It may imply that a more relaxed environment is valued, or it may speak to the busy nature of the office. The sign's intended message is implicit.

Likewise, the third level of Schein's model recognizes the hidden aspects of culture. This dimension highlights the cultural patterns that become taken for granted over time.

Underlying Assumptions

At the deepest, least tangible level of organizational culture are "underlying assumptions"—the symbols, values, and beliefs that are not clearly recognizable but continue to shape the behavior of the organization's members. Much the same way we are unaware of gravity until we fall, some parts of culture are hidden until they are made explicit.

In fact, we may not recognize this level at all. These aspects of culture are hidden in the unconscious dimensions of school life and taken for granted by those who work there. As C. A. Bowers and David J. Flinders note (1990), cultural patterns "are experienced by the individual as part of a worldview that is transparent or taken for granted."

A principal tells a parent that "buses and front gates are monitored by teachers before and immediately after school." The explicit message assures the parent that his or her student will be safe before and after school. The implicit or underlying message evokes safety as a high priority and value of the school, principal, and staff.

As the deepest level of culture, the underlying assumptions may include elements of other levels that have become taken for granted over time. For example, the administration and faculty decide on a change in policy that affects the daily schedule. Because the class period is shortened, teachers immediately recognize and feel the effects of the new policy. This noticeable change instantly becomes part of the artifacts level of culture, but as time passes the schedule develops into a daily routine. The shortened period gradually becomes a taken-for-granted practice. As the routine develops into a hidden part of the teacher's personal experience, it also becomes part of the underlying-assumptions level of culture. In this sense, the three levels are constantly fluctuating.

Culture Is Active, Not Static

Schein's three-level representation of culture is not static. The values and beliefs that guide daily interaction (second level) or the artifacts that define the most visible elements of culture (first level) may shift. They may become part of the third, or more hidden, level of culture.

Daily routines, rituals, even school architecture become part of the taken-for-granted realm of culture as time passes. Put in a new schedule for classes, remodel classrooms, or write and implement a new mission statement for the school. Teachers, students, and staff will immediately notice the changes, but as time passes what was once new becomes part of a taken-for-granted attitude. The conspicuous artifacts, values, and beliefs slip into the realm of the unconscious. The explicit becomes the implicit, and what were once easily recognizable artifacts, values, and beliefs move into the underlying-assumptions level of culture.

This fluctuation makes cultural change difficult to recognize. The need for a barometer to identify and measure culture is the subject of chapter 4.

4

IDENTIFYING AND MEASURING CULTURE

The leader who seeks to reshape a school's culture should, as a first step, try to better understand the existing culture. With this imperative in mind, we offer, in the first three sections of this chapter, some ways to identify and measure school culture at each of the three levels introduced in the previous chapter: artifacts, values and beliefs, and underlying assumptions. Next, attention turns to several instruments designed to measure school climate and culture. The final section is a reminder that, despite the many efforts to change schools, their culture remains relatively uniform and stable.

Artifacts and Change in School Culture

Teachers and administrators who are looking for a practical way of understanding school culture might first ask themselves what makes their own school unique. One thing that makes each school unique is the language and symbols used in the school. For example, to boost his students' morale, one elementary principal passes out "Dolphin Slips," which can be redeemed for prizes. In another school, a principal pairs at-risk students with "Breakfast Buddies."

List those artifacts that are significant in shaping your school's culture. Begin with the language people use in offices, classrooms, and hallways. The list doesn't have to be exhaustive but should include language heard in everyday conversation. "Use the time off as an X day" or "Cover my midterm conferences" represent just a few examples.

Don't stop with dialogue. Consider other symbols, routines, rituals, and traditions that make a school unique.

These might include the smell of the hallway, buzzers instead of bells, Snoopy Slips, rubberized asphalt playgrounds, Friday assemblies, pep rallies, parent visitation night, spring picnics, or Wednesday staff meetings. The list will never be complete and may reflect certain individual biases. But it does begin to paint a picture of school culture as expressed by the immediate effects of the climate.

The list is useful as a tool for comparison. Other schools may share some similarities or highlight differences. Talking with teachers, students, and administrators from other schools or visiting their educational facilities helps put into focus those elements that are unique to the culture of one's own school.

Another strategy for collecting artifacts is to have students and staff members write brief descriptions of the school culture. This process could be initiated by having participants describe their day or write down their feelings about school. An accumulation of written descriptions offers the principal some insight into the school's cultural ecology.

A similar idea was used by Willis J. Furtwengler and Anita Micich (1991). The authors collected symbolic pictures drawn by faculty, students, and parents from five schools. They used a small-group format at a retreat held away from the school environment. The purpose was to "make thought visible," and to identify cultural agreement among participants. This agreement was to come from drawing pictures about anything that described how people felt about their school.

The pictures were drawn and coded in seven basic areas: athletics and extracurricular activities, student life, academics, administration and authority, parents and community, school mission, and problems and issues. They were coded for frequency of appearance and for problems or concerns in each area. Coders then made comparisons between the seven categories and six cultural components—cultural leadership, quality ethic, environmental support, student membership, collaborative problem-solving, and personal and professional self-worth.

While the authors' conclusions were limited, they did discover that school members who participated in the study found it easier to communicate about issues relating to cultural leadership. This aspect alone would benefit leaders trying to address the nature of school culture at the artifacts level.

History and Change in School Culture

An original list of tangible school artifacts becomes particularly useful as one evaluates the historical changes of the institution. How artifacts change over time provides a barometer for variations in school culture. This also may be the best way to begin to understand how values and beliefs are expressed in a school setting. As the culture changes, it leaves behind a host of subtle clues.

At first these clues might appear insignificant, but even short-term observations can be important. One might consider how a list of artifacts changes over the course of a year. How do the language and symbols used at the beginning of a school year differ from those at the end? This is an important question for the practitioner, because the differences reflect pieces of a changing culture. What values and beliefs do the routines, rituals, ceremonies, and symbols communicate?

The lists themselves become more significant over the long term. A principal who understands the importance of maintaining a stable culture might consider saving lists from year to year. She might look for changes in the artifacts, such as how routines, rituals, and traditions vary, or the subtle differences in school language. The lists become a valuable resource for a more indepth assessment of school culture.

Historical relationships are important for understanding the deeper levels of school culture. Searching through old documents, minutes from past meetings, and yearbooks; looking at previously used curriculum; or talking to past employees offers the practitioner a window into the past. These activities illuminate not only the second level of school culture, but how values and beliefs are expressed over time.

The school exists as a collection of experiences and shared meanings that shape its present condition. Schools have a life. Exploring past relationships and the important symbols of school culture, one begins to understand the values and beliefs embedded in a school's life history. By looking at those variations and differences and observing how artifacts change, the principal can better comprehend the nature of school culture.

But remember: Not all elements of the school culture are visible. To better understand this dimension, we need to be aware of what is left out of our analysis.

Underlying Assumptions: Defining 'What Isn't'

The distinction between levels two and three of Schein's model is very subtle. We may recognize the values and beliefs expressed in the mission statement of a school, but the assumptions implicit in how the mission statement guides education aren't as visible.

Let's say a school changes its mission statement in response to low test scores. The new mission statement reflects a commitment to academic achievement. A historical analysis of how the mission statement had changed would highlight some of the school's important values. One might identify a value shift from breadth of coverage to academic success. That is, the focus might have shifted from equal amounts of time spent on all subjects to only those academic skills necessary for passing a test. This kind of analysis would involve the second level of Schein's model.

The underlying-assumptions level of culture focuses on how the values in the mission statement implicitly affect the direction of education. This third level prompts us to ask, "What is being left out?" In part, those beliefs and values that are left out help us identify the assumptions that implicitly define what the school considers important. A mission statement that focuses on academic achievement may leave out social needs, cooperative learning, or a liberal education. The hidden assumption of this mission statement is that academic success has a higher priority than these other values.

A school leader who aspires to be a culture builder should be concerned with "what isn't." That is, she should be concerned as much about the values and beliefs that are not highlighted as those that explicitly guide the institution. This kind of concern addresses the underlying assumptions implicit in each administrative decision.

Instruments for Measuring Climate and Culture

Instruments for assessing school culture and climate come in a bewildering array of formats, reporting procedures, and often untested psychometric properties. Most of the instruments that have been used to measure school climate focus on measuring levels of satisfaction and how people perceive the patterns of interaction and communication among the school's staff members (particularly between teachers and administrators). A few instruments, however, particularly those developed in recent years, do attempt to measure values and beliefs. Educators may even find some instruments helpful in identifying the assumptions underlying their beliefs and actions.

Nevertheless, because the terms *climate* and *culture* are often used interchangeably, and the instruments vary greatly in the phenomena they purport to measure, we have not sought to differentiate among them by our own definitions of these terms. Nor have we made an effort to classify the instruments according to Schein's three levels of culture.

Halpin and Croft's OCDQ

One of the earlier school-climate-assessment instruments was developed in 1962 by Andrew Halpin and Don Croft. Their "Organizational Climate Description Questionnaire" (OCDQ) focused on "the social interactions that occur between the teachers and the principal."

The sixty-four-item OCDQ was divided into eight subtests: four designed to measure the characteristics of the faculty as a group and four to assess the qualities associated with the principal as a leader. The group subtests were disengagement, hindrance, esprit, and intimacy. The leader subtests were aloofness, production emphasis, thrust, and consideration.

Halpin and Croft reported that school climate could be assessed along a continuum from "open" to "closed." They suggest that more open climates experienced a high level of esprit among group members and thrust by leaders. In contrast, closed climates created an inauthentic environment that featured disengagement, low esprit, and decreased production.

Despite the limited focus on just the teacher and principal, the OCDQ has its uses. As Carolyn S. Anderson (1982) points out, "The instrument has had tremendous heuristic value and has promoted a broad-based interest in school climate within elementary and secondary education."

Wayne Hoy and Sharon Clover (1986) revised the OCDQ by replacing the eight dimensions of the original OCDQ with only six dimensions—three bearing on the principal's behavior (supportive, directive, or restrictive) and three relating to the behavior of teachers (collegial, intimate, or disengaged). The authors say a pilot test revealed this schema to be more useful and accurate in characterizing school climate.

NASSP's Comprehensive Assessment of School Environments

From 1982 to 1992 the National Association of Secondary School Principals conducted a longitudinal study of school environments that suggested some important directions for school restructuring (see chapter 2). According to James W. Keefe (1993), the study identified the creation and maintenance of a positive school climate as an essential characteristic of effective schooling.

In an effort to create and assess better school environments, the NASSP developed the School Climate Survey and Student, Teacher, and Parent Satisfaction Surveys to measure student, teacher, and parent perceptions of school climate and satisfaction. These surveys are part of the Comprehensive Assessment of School Environments—Information Management System (CASE—IMS), a program that takes a systems approach to the diagnosis of school status and restructuring. As Keefe notes, "Its eight steps define the gestalt of school improvement":

1. Forming the school improvement management team
2. Raising awareness
3. Collecting baseline data
4. Comprehensive assessment
5. Interpreting data and formulating a school design statement
6. Priority setting and planning
7. Task force organization and coordination
8. Summative evaluation and reporting

These eight steps express the overarching evaluative purpose of CASE—IMS, which includes the NASSP School Climate Survey as part of this systemic approach to school restructuring.

The survey has ten scales: teacher-student relationships, security and maintenance, administration, student academic orientation, student behavioral values, guidance, student-peer relationships, parent and community-school relationships, instructional management, and student activities. James W. Keefe and Edgar A. Kelley (1990) point out that when the survey is used correctly, it identifies areas in which school climate can be improved. They offer the following example of how just two of the ten survey scales provide the practitioner with some different approaches to changing school climate:

Teacher-Student Relationships

1. Initiate or upgrade a teacher adviser program.
2. Establish teacher-student teams for the development of needed social activities, academic programs, or peer-coaching arrangements.
3. Initiate an academic-recognition program for students.
4. Identify teachers skilled in instruction or working with students and develop peer-coaching activities for teachers.
5. Help teachers select or develop classroom feedback forms to collect information from students about their perceptions and needs.

Student-Peer Relationships

1. Develop or extend the school's orientation program for new students; e.g., develop a "buddy system."
2. Schedule staff development workshops to assist teachers in planning student cooperative-learning activities.
3. Establish or improve student-recognition programs that reward cooperative and collaborative efforts by students, especially those that are cross-age, cross-SES, or cross-ethnic in nature.

These few examples, offered by Keefe and Kelley, "represent the many types of interventions that can be formulated and implemented from a review of CASE data." The CASE—IMS Climate Survey provides the practitioner with an evaluative vision for changing school climate systemically.

School Culture Assessment Questionnaire

Another recently developed instrument that can be used to identify elements of school life at the values and beliefs level is the School Culture Assessment Questionnaire (SCAQ). Designed by Marshall Sashkin and Molly G. Sashkin (1990), the questionnaire assesses the effectiveness with which an organization performs four functions: adapting to change, attaining goals, working together as a team, and sharing values and beliefs ("cultural strength"). The SCAQ can be used in conjunction with "Frames of Reference," an instrument that characterizes human behavior in an organization in terms of four perspectives: structural, political, human resources, and symbolic. According to the Sashkins, these instruments are effective in defining the "web of relationships" that exist between leaders and organizational cultures.

Other Assessment Instruments

To help school leaders choose an instrument that will provide the kind of information they want and yield the most reliable and valid data, several guides review and rate the instruments. Three of the best guides were written by Judith Arter (1987), Denise C. Gottfredson and colleagues (1986), and Ann E. Witcher (1993). The following paragraphs briefly describe three popular instruments that are reviewed by these guides.

The Effective Schools Battery (ESB) surveys students and teachers and rates thirty-four aspects of school climate. It measures morale, safety, and the general atmosphere of the school. The ESB is presented in four profiles that summarize what teachers and students report about their school.

Another instrument, the Organizational Climate Index (OCI), consists of forty true-false items. According to Witcher, "Faculty members are asked to determine if presented items are descriptive of their school." The OCI addresses six factors: intellectual climate, achievement standards, supportiveness, organizational effectiveness, orderliness, and impulse control. Results of the survey provide information about school development.

The Charles F. Kettering Ltd. School Climate Profile has been used by many schools during the past twenty-five years. The profile measures four areas of school climate: general climate factors (such as "respect," "high morale," "continuous academic and social growth," and "caring"), program determinants (such as "opportunities for active learning," "varied reward systems," and "varied learning environments"), process determinants (such as "improvement of school goals," "effective communications," "involvement in decision making," and "effective teaching-learning strategies"), and material determinants ("adequate resources," "supportive and efficient logistical system," and "suitability of school plant"). Results of the survey can provide a broad characterization of school climate.

No one model or instrument will accurately characterize all elements of a school's culture or climate. Most models illuminate the more tangible artifacts but fail to capture the entire value or belief system. Therefore, we must look to historical changes in artifacts as clues for understanding Schein's second level of culture, as explained earlier in this chapter. These historical changes reveal the values and beliefs expressed in a school setting.

The More Things Change. . .

It may sound trite, but the more things change, the more they stay the same. The LEADership Study Group acknowledges, "As an institution, public education is particularly resistant to change." So, before making an artifacts list or applying an instrument of evaluation and thinking the results are "unique," one might contemplate those elements of school culture that, by in large, have remained the same.

Thelbert L. Drake and William H. Roe (1986) suggest that many aspects of organization, teaching procedures, and learning process remain fairly consistent at schools across the United States:

1. Classes are for the most part graded rather than ungraded.
2. Students are taught each subject by a single teacher rather than by a team or series of teachers.
3. Class periods are of a uniform duration, such as 40-60 minutes.
4. The school year consists of approximately 180 days.
5. The formal school is held spring, winter, and fall and

closed during the summer months.

6. Academic subjects are given an equal amount of time throughout the school year, no matter what the subject.
7. The academic courses in the school curriculum are essentially the same.
8. The student is expected to complete four years of high school before graduation.
9. All classes begin at the beginning of the semester or school year and end at the end of the semester or school year.
10. The formal school day begins at a certain time for students and ends at a certain time for students.
11. The school building and the classroom are where formal education takes place.
12. An evaluation system, usually letter grading, is provided for pupils that compares them with the group rather than themselves.
13. Most schools have some semblance of a college preparatory, vocational education, and general-education-track system for students.
14. Students generally remain in school for 12 to 13 years.
15. Schools have a superintendent, a principal, and a teacher hierarchy.
16. All schools have a board of education and are part of a state system, and so on.

The uniformity of school structure and organization speaks to the strength of the culture and tradition in formal education. While we may think each school is unique, the reality is that in many respects schools are similar.

Thus, those attempting to understand or bring about change in school culture must realize that similarities also exist across schools. While looking for artifacts, making comparisons, researching historical backgrounds, applying instruments of evaluation, or defining "what isn't," the practitioner should not lose sight of the fact that schools actually change very little.

Keeping this self-perpetuating nature of schools in mind makes the practitioner aware that productive change is an arduous process. Reform of school culture requires persistence, patience, and a clear focus.

In the next three chapters, we offer some suggestions for transforming a school's culture. Change is possible if the leader commits to a course of action that takes advantage of the insights of systems thinking and involves all members of the school community in defining a vision for the school.

5

TRANSFORMING SCHOOL CULTURE: A SYSTEMS VIEW

In recent years, organizational analysts have been encouraging leaders of both public and private enterprises to engage in systems thinking. In simplistic terms, systems theory derives from focusing less on particulars and more on the whole. In a school culture, systems thinking might lead administrators to concentrate less on day-to-day events and more on underlying trends and forces of change.

Systems thinking inspires leaders to look closely at relationships. It also motivates them to shift the focus away from particular components of organizational management to the underlying causes and effects. Philosopher Gregory Bateson (1972), who was instrumental in the development of systems thinking, suggests that no element of the system can be separated without considering the effects on the whole. Bateson offers the following explanation:

> Thus, in no system which shows mental characteristics can any part have unilateral control over the whole. In other words, the mental characteristics of the system are immanent, not in some part, but in the system as a whole.

As practitioners seek to devise some practical strategies for change, they would do well to consider first the effects on the entire school as a system. Changing school culture may require modifications of particular components of the school, but the outcome will not be successful without a more holistic focus.

Five Principles of Systems Thinking

Peter Senge (1990), director of systems thinking and organizational learning at Massachusetts Institute of Technology, suggests that practitioners should focus on five areas in the development of a systems approach. The following five points are a synthesis of Senge's ideas as they apply to schools:

1. *Seeing interrelationships, not things, and processes, not snapshots.* Most of us have been conditioned throughout our lives to focus on things and to see the world in static images. This way of thinking leads us to accept linear explanations of systemic phenomena.

2. *Moving beyond blame.* We tend to blame each other or outside circumstances for our problems. But it is poorly designed systems, not incompetent or unmotivated individuals, that cause most organizational problems. Systems thinking shows us that there is no outside—that you and the cause of your problems are part of a single system.

3. *Distinguishing detail complexity from dynamic complexity.* Some types of complexity are more important strategically than others. Detail complexity arises from many variables of change acting at once. These variables often have a significant impact on participants. Dynamic complexity, on the other hand, looks at long-term cause and effect. The changes are more subtle and not so obvious to the participants in the system.

4. *Focusing on areas of high leverage.* Some have called systems thinking the "new dismal science" because it teaches that most obvious solutions don't work—at best, they improve matters in the short run, only to make things worse in the long run. But there is another side to the story. Systems thinking also shows that small, well-focused actions can produce significant, enduring improvements, if they are in the right place. Systems thinkers refer to this idea as the principle of "leverage." Tackling a difficult problem is often a matter of seeing where the high leverage lies, where a change—with a minimum of effort—would lead to lasting, significant improvement.

5. *Avoiding symptomatic solutions.* The pressures to intervene in school cultures that are dysfunctional can be overwhelming. Unfortunately, given the linear thinking that predominates in most schools (and society in general),

interventions usually focus on symptomatic fixes, not underlying causes. This results in only temporary relief, and it tends to create still more pressures later on for further low-level intervention.

Senges' principles of systems thinking are evident in the following discussion of qualities that define an effective work culture.

Correlates of an Effective Culture

Culture is "the key to administrative practice and organizational improvement," say William Cunningham and Donn Gresso. They contend that structural reforms like site-based management will not improve schools in the absence of a supportive culture. "Effective cultures interact with structure to produce organizations of high morale, productivity and quality."

Their book *Cultural Leadership: The Culture of Excellence in Education* is a synthesis of findings and wisdom derived primarily from the Danforth Foundation's School Administrators Fellowship Program, which launched and studied the progress of improvement plans in forty-two school districts over six years.

Drawing from the experiences of these school districts and other research, Cunningham and Gresso describe correlates or conditions that, when occurring together, "allow the organization to develop the most effective and efficient work culture. These become the basic tenets that guide the work of administrators, regardless of the level at which they work." Only when these correlates are present can such strategies as participative decision-making, site-based management, total quality management, and programs for a learning organization succeed.

The value of teamwork is a recurrent theme that runs through the correlates of an effective culture summarized below.

1. *The Vertical Slice.* A team of individuals across all levels of an organization meets regularly to communicate diverse views and values and to address issues of interest. In a school district, the team might include a school board member, the superintendent, a principal, a teacher, a secretary, a parent, and a student, operating with the help of

a well-trained facilitator. The ongoing interaction of team members helps to establish "a vertical culture that crosses over all of the horizontal cultures within the organization."

2. *Vision, Not Deficiencies.* Unlike the deficit model, where the focus is on identifying and solving problems, the visionary model focuses the team's attention on defining what school should be like and then exerting the effort to achieve the ideal.

3. *Collegial Relationships.* "Team members cannot work toward a desired outcome until they have formed a sense of community or team spirit and learned to trust and support one another." Cunningham and Gresso stress that collegiality means mutual ownership of both problems and visions; one party cannot create a vision at the expense of another.

4. *Trust and Support.* For a team to work effectively, the members must understand and trust one another. "Trust develops," say the authors, "as we understand people's values and interests, where they are coming from and why they take a given position."

5. *Values and Interest, Not Power and Position.* So that decisions are not the result of a battle of wills, the team members should put aside their rank and focus on their values and interests. "The role of the leader is to reconcile interests rather than develop compromises among positions."

6. *Access to Quality Information.* Besides being a major source of power in an organization, accurate information is useful in building a common culture, enabling the work group to make sound decisions, and giving each employee feedback for improving his or her performance.

7. *Broad Participation.* The group's diversity of values, beliefs, knowledge, and interests is its strength. When all members participate and contribute their talents, the group derives a synergistic effect that is greater than if the individuals worked independently of one another.

8. *Lifelong Growth.* Through resources and encouragement, the organization helps each individual sustain a process of inquiry and self-development. In this way, "employees constantly redefine themselves and what they are capable of doing."

9. *Individual Empowerment.* Individuals who have come to depend on others for direction cannot develop their full potential. This loss of potential among all the members is

the difference between effective and ineffective organizations. For employees to be free and empowered to take risks and make a difference, the organizational culture must enable the uniqueness of each individual "to unfold and flow."

10. *Continuous and Sustained Innovation.* Achievement of a collective vision requires a long-term, concerted effort. Therefore, "school improvement is a cultural, ongoing, cumulative process," say Cunningham and Gresso, not a series of quick fixes. "Effective cultures invite and support continuous improvement from within rather than externally developed reform and restructuring efforts."

Cunningham and Gresso shed much light on what is required to transform a school's culture so that it can sustain innovation and improvement. Culture building is more than telling a few stories at faculty meetings and promoting a new motto for the school. It is a process that cuts deeply into the fabric of people's relationships, their patterns of communication and interaction, and their regard for their own potential as well as that of the organization they serve. An excellent culture is the net result of the activities of individuals who are themselves, both on their own and as members of a work group, growing in identity, confidence, knowledge, cooperation, commitment, and respect.

CASE—IMS School Improvement Process

NASSP's Comprehensive Assessment of School Environments Model offers not only a research-validated instrument for assessing school climate (see chapter 4), but also a systemic process for redesigning the school environment (Howard and Keefe 1994). The CASE—IMS school-improvement process uses the results of the CASE—IMS assessment instrument.

The process starts with a school design statement that outlines the specifications for a desired school of the future. According to Howard and Keefe, "The design statement provides the direction and focus for the school's planned change process."

The twelve-step design statement begins with three basic components: a mission statement; a compilation of philosophical, psychological, and organizational assumptions; and a student-outcomes statement. These features give the school vision and purpose. They provide the core elements of the new school design.

The other nine elements of the design statement are referred to as system components. These components address the more pragmatic and practical elements of the school-restructuring effort. The nine components include curricula and instructional programs; instructional techniques; school structure and organization; school culture and climate; school leadership, management, and budgeting; school staffing and staff development; communication and political structures; school resources, physical plant, and equipment; and evaluation plan. In Howard and Keefe's words, "All twelve components are essential to a successfully restructuring school."

Once the design statement is complete, it acts as a template for the school organization and a roadmap for managing changes in school culture.

Changing Artifacts—A Systems View

The previous chapter suggested using artifacts as a way to gauge and understand change in school cultures. An effort to change artifacts works best when the leader has an appreciation for the system and its web of cultural relationships. Traditions, rituals, daily routines, schedules, and ceremonies can all be implemented or changed; without an appreciation for how the changes affect the entire system, however, the outcome may not be what the leader intended.

Changes in climate and cultural artifacts must be acted on with extreme care, especially if the leader is coming into a new environment. People become attached to the traditions and rituals that make up school life. Altering or modifying these traditions without regard for people's feelings about them may cause anxiety or antagonism. Any reform in the current system should incorporate the views and perspectives of all those affected by the change.

Let's consider how the systems view might guide a principal who wants to change one of his school's most visible artifacts. Principal Glen Thompson wanted to expand the role of school assemblies. In the past, school assemblies focused primarily on athletic events. Cheerleaders rooted for the team, and coaches and players gave inspirational speeches. Thompson saw a need to include the value of academic success, but he didn't want to disrupt past traditions. So he formed a committee of students and teachers to look into expanding the role of school assemblies to include academic success. The committee met several times and then recommended a gradual process of recognizing student achievement. At first assemblies began by recognizing athletes with outstanding scholastic accomplishments. By the end of the year, all students in high academic standing were considered for awards.

In this case, the artifact considered for change was the school assembly. Principal Thompson took a systemic approach to changing the artifact by (1) employing a process of gradual change, and (2) relying on the input of faculty and students. The outcome worked for everyone involved. Thompson was able to emphasize the value of academic success, and teachers and students were able to keep what they felt was an important school tradition.

Glen Thompson's action illustrates the impact a principal's leadership can have. That leadership is also critical in orchestrating the development of a vision for the school.

6

TRANSFORMING SCHOOL CULTURE: SHARED VISION

"It is not, as we commonly believe, that the past plus the present form our vision of the future; rather the past plus our vision of the future form the present."

Phillip Schlechty

Principal Jack Thomas has a vision of what he wants Mount Day Elementary School to look like in five years. The vision includes higher student achievement, increased teacher motivation, and more parent involvement. Thomas is committed to perfecting a school culture that is both efficient and productive. In the past, Mount Day has suffered from high student dropout rates and increased numbers of burned-out teachers. Class sizes grow larger each year, but the thin, windowless hallways provide no relief for students or staff.

Low mileage for midforties, Thomas is the picture of professionalism. He arrives each morning at 6:00 a.m. in a suit, tie, and cupped Wing Tips. Teachers and office staff address him as "Jack," but in front of students he is always "Mr. Thomas" or "Principal Thomas." "The idea," says Jack, "is to create an atmosphere of mutual respect." To that end, Principal Thomas spends much of his time developing new programs that promote his vision of school success. That vision includes achievement, productivity, staff efficiency, and goal-setting in an environment of respect and consideration for others.

Upon the recommendation of a colleague, Principal Thomas instituted a program designed to boost student morale. The program was called "Day Lights," and its purpose was to recognize the "bright moments" in a student's day at Mount Day Elementary. Awards were given to students by teachers or other staff members any time the children initiated behavior that promoted a more positive school culture or climate. A six-page handout and a weekly staff meeting were devoted solely to the Day Lights program. The awards were intended to promote Principal Thomas's vision of higher achievement, respect, and productivity at school.

Teachers were required to keep track of student awards. For each ten awards, a letter was sent to parents congratulating them on their student's outstanding behavior. Each day became a new challenge for staff, as they had to mark, count, calculate, and recognize new Day Lights winners. The process became so labor intensive that teachers complained: "It took more time to calculate the stupid awards than to prepare for a week of class."

Eventually, the new program failed. But it failed only after three months of contentious debate about the program between the principal and staff. Staff meetings flared with comments about the workload and questions about the real benefit to students. Teachers expressed anger; Principal Thomas felt unsupported; and in the end parents and students wondered what the point was of the Day Lights program. But perhaps the biggest loser was the school's culture. It seemed to suffer the most because Jack Thomas failed to recognize that a vision must be shared by all members of the organization.

Principal Thomas discovered that although theoretically an organizational vision can bind people together, without consensus a vision can also destroy organizational culture. Thomas was blinded by what he thought school should look like. In the process, the school culture turned hostile and unproductive, just the opposite of what the principal intended.

This fictitious example illustrates the most important lesson of change in any school culture: The creation of a school's vision must be a collaborative activity. The crucial question, says Michael G. Fullan (1992), dean of education at the University of Toronto, is "Whose vision is it?" "Principals," he says, "are blinded by their own vision when they feel they must manipulate the teachers and the school culture to conform to it." A more useful approach is to make "vision building a collective exercise."

Creating Shared Responsibility

As Fullan points out, the process of negotiating a shared vision of school culture should be *collaborative*, more than just cooperative. The idea isn't to make staff members cooperate with the principal's vision; rather, it is to give all members of the organization the opportunity to help create the vision. In this way, everyone shares the responsibility for culture building.

The principles encompassed in a vision provide the most positive direction and energy for an organization when they are shared by the work group. As we noted in the previous chapter, Cunningham and Gresso include the visionary model of planning on their list of the correlates of an effective culture. They say "the shared vision serves as the bonding agent within the culture." It is the glue that holds together and unifies the aspirations, commitments, and interests of the organization's members around common themes and shared purposes. The vision is what communicates to members of the work group what is worth doing and how. Obviously, the more committed members are to the vision, the harder they will work together to attain the vision.

Paradoxically, the vision binds together and solidifies the work culture, giving it purpose and unity, but the vision is also the product of an effective work culture. To create a vision, the organization's members must listen to one another, feel empowered to change the organization, have confidence in their ability to improve their performance, think critically and gather data about where the organization is at present, and hold strong convictions about the ideals that should guide their work in the future. These are all characteristics of an effective work culture. Such a culture is fertile soil for the continual generation and germination of new ideas about what the organization can accomplish. Indeed, the power of the vision-building process derives from the fact that it is ongoing; it is the way a productive work group continually challenges itself to recreate the future—and therefore change the present.

Guidelines for Creating a Vision

There is no one particular strategy or set of steps every school should take to define its vision. Shoes come in different sizes, and so do vision-creating processes. The strategy each school chooses will conform to its own particular style of decision-making and the level of maturity of its work culture. If staff members are not used to working as a team, for example, some preliminary effort will probably have to be devoted to training in group-process skills. Rather than prescribe one size to fit all, we offer the following principles to guide the vision-building process.

1. *Involve all stakeholders.* The strength of a work culture is measured by the degree to which all members of the work team believe in and strive to achieve the organization's vision. For this reason, the vision-building process is also a community-building process. When the principal and all teachers and other staff members share with one another their dreams and ideals and begin to trust one another, they forge a bond that will withstand the trials they will encounter in putting their vision into practice.

2. *Follow your dreams.* The present reality may be comfortable or it may be intolerable. Complacency is the enemy of inspiration just as frustration and anger make us too willing to welcome change of any kind. A vision captures an ideal state of affairs. It attracts and inspires us precisely because it is truly what we long for, what promises to yield the greatest sense of fulfillment.

3. *Inform your ideals with data; commit to continual learning.* Many vision-building teams conduct research to gain a more exact understanding of what an effective school looks like. Equally important is ongoing professional development to help staff members sharpen their instructional skills and learn about school-improvement strategies. Employees whose knowledge and skills are constantly improving more eagerly face the challenges of the future.

4. *Assign tasks to work teams.* Everyone participates equally in definition of the vision, but the steps of implementation can be delegated to smaller groups. For example, a school planning team could be charged with writing the vision statement that expresses the community's ideals. That or another team could then develop a first-year plan of action. Other groups could plan needed professional development and devise strategies for any major changes, such as adoption of a new curriculum.

5. *Live the vision.* As Cunningham and Gresso say, "If the vision needs to be written in order to be communicated, there is no shared vision." The vision affects the life of the school only when its ideals are internalized, when it becomes written in people's hearts and minds. These two authors write:

As the mission becomes a part of the work culture, the work group begins to operate in a highly aligned manner. The group knows what needs to be done and can sense when convergence and synergy is being achieved. Employees talk until they can each tell they are seeing things in the same way. There is little need for formal statements of agreement, as agreement is understood. At this point, the work culture has achieved a deep level of understanding that will propagate throughout the organization.

6. *Tap the power of symbols to communicate the vision.* Stories, logos, mottos, meaningful names for physical features (How about "Commitment Courtyard," "Attitude Alley"?), murals, assemblies, and symbolic actions by key personnel are valuable devices for drawing attention to the school's core values. Beware, however, of using symbols in an advertising blitz to persuade people to think or act differently. To inspire allegiance to a vision, symbols must remind people of values they already believe in, by virtue of having been involved in the definition of the school's vision.

7. *Commit to an ongoing process.* Creating a vision within an organization is not a static event, because people and institutions change. As Peter Senge notes, "At any one point there will be a particular image of the future that is predominant, but that image will evolve." Vision-building is a never-ending process of incremental adjustments. If a school expresses its vision as a five-year projection into the future, then each year or at least every other year the personnel will revise their vision on the basis of current knowledge and aspirations.

The Principal's Role

No one should fault a principal for arriving at a school with a preconceived vision of what that school ought to become. After all, the principal's strongly held convictions about educational goals and outcomes probably figured heavily in the superintendent's decision to assign the principal to that school. The question for the principal now becomes How much should I push my own vision?

We suggest that principals who are in this situation listen to the advice of one of their colleagues. Nancy Wilson, a principal of fifteen years, at the time of this writing assigned to Boekman Creek Elementary School in Wilsonville, Oregon, suggests that the best way to approach changes in school culture initially is to "do nothing." Her advice is to "talk to teachers, talk to staff, and learn something about the culture you're in first." Take time to thoroughly understand the organization. Then and only then, a principal can begin to approach change by empowering staff and negotiating a shared vision.

If a leader starts with a preconceived vision, he or she should proceed with extreme caution. As a person in a position of power, the principal may place students and staff members in an uncomfortable position. They may feel an obligation to conform to the principal's wishes and may regard disagreement as a threat to their job security or personal status.

Facilitating the Vision Process

A principal's reticence to propose his or her own vision is wise for the reason we have stressed throughout this chapter: For any vision, no matter who proposes it, to make a difference, all members of the work group must rally around it. A principal who appreciates the need for vision to drive a strong work culture knows that the power of a vision comes not just from the soundness of its ideas but from the unity of purpose that is achieved when all members believe in, claim as their own, and act on that vision.

There are many paths to excellence; what is indispensable is teamwork once a particular path has been chosen. Viewed in this light, the principal's role is best seen not as originator of the vision but as facilitator of the vision.

Another way to put it is that the principal's personal vision ought simply to be that everyone in the school *agree* on a vision. Rather than control the specifics of the vision, the principal facilitates the process by which all teachers, aides, office staff, custodians, parents, and students decide on their common vision. The leader's role is to smooth the way and garner the support and resources for such a consensus to be realized.

The principal must have the same priorities as a successful football coach, who knows that winning games depends less on whether the offense lines up in the wishbone or pro-set formation than on how thoroughly the players under-stand the type of offense that is used and play effectively as a team. The difference is that a football coach chooses the type of offense and then on the practice field instills teamwork, whereas the principal involves everyone in the choice because, in a school, it is the only way to build a team. As facilitator, the principal communicates trust that all members of the school community are as committed to excellence as he or she is.

Perhaps the best way to begin is to encourage an atmo-sphere where staff and students feel comfortable offering visionary ideas. Principal Bob Anderson of North Eugene High School does that by creating a safe environment where staff feel inclined to participate. According to Lynn Balster Liontos, he does this through:

> (1) his strong sense of caring, (2) his openness and ap-proachability, (3) his ability to let people know that it's okay to disagree with him, (4) his encouragement of risk-taking and trying new ideas, (5) his ability to allow people to feel it's okay to make mistakes or fail, and (6) his strong support for staff.

Many times students and staff remain outside the cre-ative process. Bob Anderson demonstrates that by paying attention to the values and interests of all members of the organization, the principal can better facilitate a shared vision.

Blending Internal and External Demands

Culture goes beyond the front doors of the school. In the same sense, visions are not confined to what happens in classrooms, hallways, and front offices. A school's vision must satisfy a variety of external demands, such as meeting the academic goals of the school district, responding to community needs and parent requests, and complying with state and federal legal requirements.

These outside influences all play a role in shaping the school's vision, with a force that is at least equal to the internal needs of the educational environment that center on student and staff relationships. The principal is in the best position to orchestrate the blending of these various internal and external elements into a coherent and accepted shared vision.

Learning from Failure

Possibly the toughest job for any leader is admitting failure. If Principal Jack Thomas had learned this lesson before initiating his Day Lights program, he probably would have had more success at Mount Day Elementary. Learning from failure is an act of personal reflection. An administrator should always consider how his or her actions affect the current organizational culture. Several important questions arise: How does the process of change influence others? Where does the principal or administrator fit into the process? What are all the possible outcomes of organizational change? and What happens when irreconcilable differences arise? Reflecting on these questions may be the most important task of a successful leader of change.

When changes undertaken to improve a school's culture do not have their intended result, what is a leader to do? Stop, reevaluate, and try again is certainly one option. But the solution may be as simple as helping people adjust to the change with some words of encouragement. In situations where consensus is unattainable, the leader may resort to cultivating the value of peaceful coexistence. Rather than force agreement, sometimes it is best to acknowledge that people may not share the same values but still can find a way to work together harmoniously.

Failure of one kind or another is an inevitable part of life. What a vision offers is a beacon to guide the leader and the school to rediscover their way once it has been lost. And once the values expressed in the vision permeate the organizational culture, the likelihood of failure diminishes, as the members' actions become aligned with the vision.

7

TRANSFORMING SCHOOL CULTURE: THE ROLE OF THE LEADER

"Culture-building requires that school leaders give attention to the informal, subtle and symbolic aspects of school life which shape the beliefs and actions of each employee within the system. The task of leadership is to create and support the culture necessary to foster an attitude of effectiveness in everything that is done within the school. Once this attitude is achieved and supported by the culture, all other aspects of the organization will fall in line. This is why culture-building is the key to organizational success."

William G. Cunningham and Don W. Gresso

In this final chapter, we examine more closely the leader's role as a culture builder. Whereas the previous two chapters discussed the need for the leader to adopt a systems perspective and involve all members of the school community in designing its vision, the focus of this chapter is on the leader as learner, motivator, and modeler. We also suggest some strategies and activities school principals can draw upon in transforming their school's culture.

Three cautions are called for. First, the strategies we have selected are by no means intended to be exhaustive. The range of options a culture builder may employ is extremely broad, a reflection of the complexity and breadth of the phenomenon of culture. Second, as we have emphasized in chapter 5 and elsewhere, cultural transformation is a systemic, organic process. Implementation of a few isolated activities, perhaps with the intention of helping teachers and students feel good about their school, will not likely have a lasting or significant impact on the school's culture.

And finally, when we consider the self-perpetuating nature of organizational culture and consider further that the principal is a member of the school's organization, it is reasonable to ask whether the principal's power to change a school's culture is greater than the culture's power to change the principal. Some authors have argued in the negative. In their view, a principal's efforts to significantly change school culture can only lead to frustration and defeat. Others argue (and we are among them) that the power of leadership should not be ignored. Martin L. Maehr and Stephanie A. Parker (1993) remind us that "leaders are not simply the captives of culture. They can and do affect it."

The actual power of the principal to influence the culture of a school lies somewhere between inefficacy and total responsibility. The principal is indeed subject to the norms and other socializing forces of the school. As Ron Renchler (1992) notes,

> The dynamics and logistics of most schools are such that the principal cannot possibly oversee the motivational needs of each and every student. But groups of people can be affected by the culture in which they participate, and this domain is under the control and stewardship of the principal.

In the process, principals must continuously guard against feelings of complacency or self-validating futility.

According to Edgar Schein (1985), "Leadership is intertwined with culture formation." Developing an organizational culture and shaping the creative process of its evolution is the "unique and essential function" of leadership. Nevertheless, the principal alone cannot bring about change in the norms of a school because, by definition, cultural transformation is a collaborative activity. The principal must engage others both inside and outside the school if he or she is to effect any meaningful changes in the school's culture.

Before we consider the practical steps principals can take, the next section spells out a model for rethinking the leader's role.

New Leadership Roles

The traditional view of a leader as an authoritarian decision-maker is obsolete. True, leaders must at times make unpopular and difficult decisions, but they should do so in a collaborative process. To qualify as culture builders in today's schools, administrators ought to take a second look at how they approach leadership. Peter Senge (1990) offers a three-fold model for rethinking leadership roles. These critical roles are seeing the leader as designer, teacher, and steward.

Reforming leadership styles can be a difficult process. The change requires a recognition of power relationships between the principal and other members of the school. It also demands attention, by the principal, to current roles and decision-making processes. But the most important prerequisite is a willingness to relinquish some authority and control over the administrative and creative processes.

Leader as Designer

Making change possible may be the best way to describe the leader's role as designer. Adopting a design framework means gaining an understanding of the administrative avenues best suited for change. In other words, the leader knows how to put a vision or plan into action. This doesn't mean that a leader must always have a rational plan or strategy. To the contrary, a leader should be continually learning and trying new strategies that make an "emergent phenomenon" possible.

The leader as designer understands the creative process of transforming a plan or vision into reality. Leaders should cultivate the following skills in their quest to become better designers: (1) having a workable familiarity with bureaucratic processes; (2) knowing how to translate a vision or idea into a policy; (3) being able to reconceptualize the change ("How will the change look?"); and (4) understanding the persuasive strategies necessary to bring groups together in the process of change.

When operating within the design framework, the leader will adopt a "tight" leadership style, as explained by Peggy Odell Gonder and Donald Hymes (1994). Tight leadership involves communication of institutional values and beliefs. Principals entrusted with navigating the waters of institutional change must pay attention to where the ship is headed. Once the direction of reform is lost or institutional values are not communicated effectively, the organization begins to drift without a clear course. People in such an organization feel lost or frustrated by the lack of leadership. The principal navigates by directing the communication that helps all members of the organization understand and put into action the organization's values and beliefs.

In contrast, "loose" leadership styles permit a certain amount of autonomy within the organization; they free people to act independently. Gonder and Hymes argue that the principal should adopt a flexible leadership style, both loose—allowing for personal autonomy—and tight—directing the communication of values and beliefs that give purpose to institutional change.

Leader as Teacher

"Leader as teacher does not mean leader as authoritarian expert whose job it is to teach people the 'correct' view of reality," says Senge. The role of leader as teacher is, rather, about helping everyone in the school organization, including the leader himself or herself, to gain more perceptive and insightful views of reality. This view of teaching has more in common with facilitating, guiding, or coaching. The leader as teacher should be most concerned with the negotiation of boundaries.

C. A. Bowers and David J. Flinders (1990) describe the process of negotiation as defining "what is." They explain, "Recognizing and negotiating these boundaries involves foremost a cultural understanding of supervision that sensitizes supervisors to the metamessages communicated by nonverbal cues and to patterns of thought generated by metaphor." That is, the leader as teacher needs to pay attention to the language essential for establishing the boundaries of cultural change.

Deal and Peterson use the example of Bob Mastruzzi, principal of Kennedy High School in New York City, to describe how using conflict can build consensus. This example also describes how a leader helps negotiate a shared sense of meaning:

> Conflict arose between the school and the community when local adults complained of student disruptions. Mastruzzi demonstrated his understanding of diverse cultures and his political acumen through his measured

response to fierce community objections (with racial overtones) about the "hordes" of students marching through the neighborhood from the subway station to school each morning. Through negotiation and persuasion he secured commitment from the city to widen the side walks.

Mastruzzi framed conflicts between faculty and administration and between the community and the school in terms of an underlying shared sense of mission and accomplishment. At the least, Mastruzzi made sure that faculty and community members understood the values of the school and what it was trying to achieve.

Bill Mastruzzi exemplifies the leader as teacher. He facilitates a process of negotiation by framing conflict in a language that defines "what is." He establishes clear boundaries and allows participants to reach agreement that reflects the core values of the community. In this way, people feel a sense of empowerment and take ownership of goals they help to define.

Becoming a leader as teacher requires the principal to pay attention to language, both verbal and nonverbal. This process, according to Senge, includes (1) framing the boundaries of discussion, defining "what is"; (2) remembering a shared sense of values in the negotiation process; (3) recognizing moments for bringing forward the implicit elements of discussion (such as administrative processes, historical contexts, traditional practices, or cultural differences); and (4) making all participants aware of the frameworks used to guide the dialogue.

Leader as Steward

Stewardship may be the subtlest form of leadership, according to Senge. The leader as steward is defined by an attitude. While stewardship has long been recognized as a style of leadership, its form has not been clearly defined. Stewardship combines elements of commitment and compassion. In the words of Senge, the steward as leader operates on two levels: "stewardship for the people they lead and stewardship for the larger purpose or mission that underlies the enterprise." Neither is more important than the other.

The key lies in understanding that these two elements always work together.

The first—stewardship for people—arises from an appreciation for the impact of one's leadership on others. "People can suffer economically, emotionally, and spiritually under inept leadership," Senge says. The principal who recognizes the impact of his or her decisions and expresses compassion for other members of the school culture will be a more effective leader. This appreciation should instill a sense of responsibility in leaders.

The second element of stewardship comes from an understanding of the larger mission or purpose of the school. People sense when leaders lose interest or direction. The administrator is responsible for the aims implicit in the values and policies of the institution. Stewardship makes the enactment of this mission an act of both compassion and commitment.

Reflection and Dialogue

"The very first place to begin change," writes Michael Fullan (1994), "is within ourselves." Cultural change begins only when practitioners address the process of reform personally. This means setting personal goals as well as institutional goals, becoming immersed in the process of change, paying attention to what is happening in the organization, and learning to enjoy the immediate experience.

Fullan uses the term *inner-learning* to characterize the personal transformations that must take place for an organization to change. A systemic transformation starts personally with self-talk. Concerned administrators reevaluate and question each important successful institutional change. As Fullan notes, "Sorting out one's own individual stance toward improvement is just as important as deciding on collective response."

Outer-learning, Fullan says, has to do with the connections we make with others. Practitioners involved in organizational change realize the importance of collaborative efforts. Building these relationships takes effort and a genuine concern for those involved in the process. "Collaboration takes time," writes Charlotte a' Campo (1993), "time to meet, plan together and visit each other." These relationships form the basis of outer-learning. People must learn about the change process together and learn to act with a common purpose in mind.

Together, inner- and outer-learning are fairly simple concepts. Inner-learning builds on self-reflection and personal goals. Outer-learning combines these ideas with collaborative relationships. We work together for systemic change, but that change can't happen until we've made a personal commitment to change. Fullan concludes that "systems change when enough kindred spirits coalesce in the same change direction."

In a similar vein, Lee G. Bolman and Terrence E. Deal (1994) say that some of the most important lessons in the process of cultural change come from staff, parents, students, and teachers. Too often leaders get caught up in the macropolitics of organizational change, and they fail to listen to or consider individual voices. Bolman and Deal advise leaders to take these voices more seriously. The authors contend that "many managers or leaders learn too little— or learn the wrong things—from what happens to them. Effective learning often requires individual reflection or peer discussions to distill important lessons from life experiences."

Self-reflection can be enhanced by feedback. The school leader should take the time to pursue others' opinions, perhaps even create a formal mechanism for dialogue and feedback such as meetings, retreats, and suggestion boxes. "Standing back from the situation and disentangling complex causes and effects," say Bolman and Deal, "can play an important role in figuring out what to do differently in the next situation." The leader who chooses to listen and reflect on the suggestions of colleagues will likely manage the process of change better. This is a crucial step in creating an environment open to cultural change.

Using Narrative

Storytelling is one way for a principal to influence cultural change. As Deal and Peterson note, "It can show the listeners, the school community, what the principal values without direct moralizing."

A good storyteller builds a relationship with the listener by choosing a story that has an associative quality. For instance, a story about classroom life might be more appropriate for a teacher than a truck driver. The teacher relates more closely with the experience of teaching in a classroom. A principal who chooses a story that fits the person and the occasion will be more effective in communicating shared values and beliefs.

The values implicit in the story often go unrecognized by the listener. Many times, the storyteller must facilitate the process by interpreting what values and beliefs are integral to the story. Consider the following example, a story told about a teacher, Phil MacCullum, who was giving a lecture on the Boston Tea Party to his class of fifth graders:

> Phil, a large boisterous man with a silvery mustache, captivates his students with an exciting tale. So much so, they seem to genuinely lose themselves in the description of the Colonists' rebellious act. "In the dead of night, dressed as Native American warriors with tomahawks and face paint, they dumped the crates of tea into the Boston Harbor," he tells his students in a low and intense voice. He pauses and the classroom steeps in silence. The students' eyes are wide. From the back of the room a small uncertain hand rises for a question. "Yes, Eric, what is it?," Phil inquires, commanding the attention of the entire class. A genuinely concerned Eric asks, "Have they been caught yet?"

This story could be used in a number of different ways. The interpretation might focus on the power of a good teacher to captivate students and excite them about learning. The story could facilitate a discussion of the differences between teacher intent and student comprehension. Or the storyteller might expand on the value of protest for a worthy cause. There are many possibilities.

The principal can use the power of a story to germinate and spread the important values of the institution. Principal Joan Andrews uses a story about Marty Matthews to relieve first-year teachers of their anxiety about teaching.

> No one in your room this year is like Marty. Marty was a bit of a hyperactive kid. I think his parents even had him on Ritalin to control his behavior. Anyway, I was a young first-year teacher when I had Marty, and I was quite nervous about doing everything just right. I did my lesson plans two weeks in advance and my bulletin boards three weeks before school started. I was very careful that year

about setting a consistent example. At the first sign of trouble, I sent kids down to the vice principal's office.

Marty was making clucking sounds all through silent reading and had adamantly protested when I asked him to be quiet. True to my word, I sent Marty to the vice principal for the rest of the day. Well, the next day in class, Marty had drafted a petition that he was having every student sign. The petition read, "Sign Here If You Hate Mrs. Andrews." You can imagine how I felt, but these are just the lessons of a first-year teacher. (Betty Seigrist, personal communication, January 14, 1994)

Andrews uses this story to relate a number of different values—expressing support for teachers, finding humor in difficult situations, setting consistent examples in the classroom, and emphasizing the importance of experience. The story provides a template for understanding school life. Two critical elements of the story-telling process are to (1) use stories with an associative quality, and (2) facilitate or direct the interpretive process. Effective use of narrative can help principals build stronger institutional cultures.

William A. Firestone and Bruce L. Wilson (1993) suggest making use of "old-timers" to communicate the values of the institution. Past employees and older graduates can recite narratives of the school's history, thus serving as role models to the uninitiated. "They establish a positive link with the newcomers that builds ownership and pride in the school." These old-timers may also play a key role in establishing or reestablishing important rituals and ceremonies.

Organization of the School Day

Scheduling may seem like a small factor in determining school culture, but in practice it may be one of the biggest. Consider that the scheduling of the school day affects almost all school activities. It determines how students are grouped, how they use their free time, and what choices they make. The same conditions apply to teachers. Scheduling affects how teachers plan lessons, what they do with their free time, and where they see themselves in the organization. In fact, say Martin L. Maehr and Rachel M. Buck (1993), "Action in these areas is critical to determining and transforming the culture of the school and is an important way in which the learning and motivation of students is influenced."

Maehr and Buck use the forty- to fifty-minute class period as an example. They suggest that this type of class is well suited for more rigid didactic instruction. Schools interested in project-centered instruction would probably want to consider a longer class period. This would allow for instruction beyond the school walls and would help students and teachers develop and understand projects more fully.

We are not suggesting that one form of scheduling is better than another. Rather, the illustration emphasizes the importance of coordinating schedules with the values important to the institution. More flexible institutions would want to choose more flexible schedules. Likewise, a more traditional emphasis in the classroom would function better with a more traditional schedule. But these are choices that must be addressed by the principal and staff.

Setting a Consistent Example

Actions speak loudest. The most effective and efficient way to change cultures is to model the behaviors, beliefs, and values important to the institution. A principal who acts with care and concern for all will most likely encourage similar behavior in those around him or her. Likewise, a principal who has little time for staff or students will participate in creating a selfish culture.

Modeling sets an example. People see and feel the behaviors of others. The principal who leads by action makes beliefs and values of the institution highly visible and inspires others to follow his or her example.

Staff Development

Staff development is a time-honored method of cultural change in schools. Not only the content of staff development but also the manner in which it is delivered can communicate desired values. Kenneth Leithwood and Doris Jantzi (1990) contend that "staff development which acknowledges what can be learned from one's immediate colleagues, as well as others, fosters a collaborative culture and is, in turn, nurtured by that same culture."

Principals can foster staff development in both direct and indirect ways. First, principals can act directly by giving workshops in their areas of expertise. During these seminars, school leaders may communicate or model important values. Workshop lessons could even be constructed around a particular ceremony or ritual.

Second, principals can act indirectly by informing their staffs of inservice opportunities and encouraging participation. By staying informed of the types of inservice available, principals can make wise suggestions about which programs best suit the needs of a changing school culture.

Mary Lynn Hamilton and Virginia Richardson (1995) conclude that the interaction between school culture and staff development affects progress toward group collaboration and teacher empowerment.

Selecting Compatible Staff

Perhaps one of the principal's toughest yet most vital tasks is selecting staff members who share his or her values and beliefs about education. There is nothing more counterproductive to creating a healthy school culture than for the faculty and principal to hold incompatible convictions about what schooling should be. A principal who is mindful of culture-building seeks faculty members who are not only technically qualified but whose values are consistent with the principal's vision of excellence.

Effective school leaders go to great lengths to build a cohesive faculty, using the processes of recruitment, selection, and induction to shape their schools' culture. They not only carefully recruit and select new faculty, but they help teachers who do not share their values to find positions at other schools. They use the selection interview as an opportunity to clearly communicate the school's culture to each candidate. And after they hire a teacher, they socialize the new faculty member into the core values of the school.

All five principals profiled by Deal and Peterson agreed that "getting the right staff" is an essential component in the creation of a healthy school culture. Frank Boyden of

Massachusetts' Deerfield Academy went so far as to say he was "delighted when a teacher turned down a more highly paid job" to remain at his school. This was a signal to him that the values of the institution were more important than money or status, and he often used instances of teachers' declining better paying job offers as examples in stories.

Recognizing Staff Members

Daily life in an organization has peaks and valleys. Teachers know the highs and lows of classroom instruction. One day can be a celebration of high test scores and student cooperation. The next day can be a futile struggle to maintain order and teach basic skills. The competent teacher takes both days in stride.

An insightful leader recognizes the importance of these peaks and valleys. Peaks provide an opportunity to celebrate accomplishments, and valleys call for some timely encouragement.

Recognition of faculty members must be both significant and genuine. Its aim is both to improve staff morale and to draw attention to an important value, such as high expectations for student achievement.

Informal and formal recognition of staff members can be expressed in a number of ways, say Gonder and Hymes. Principals can show informal appreciation "through notes and positive comments, both privately and in staff meetings." At a time of low morale, how about planning a breakfast or dinner event to recognize teachers with humorous and/or serious awards? In the age of electronic media, principals can use e-mail to deliver positive comments.

A method of formal recognition is to recommend teachers for district, state, and national awards. Principals can talk to district officials about establishing new awards or nominate teachers for those already available. Local papers and school publications can also be used to celebrate the hard work of teachers.

Lessons for the Principal

Jane Arkes of George Middle School in Portland, Oregon,

says, "The toughest lesson for any principal is learning to be patient." In her career, she has seen many good school leaders come and go. "The reason is often the same: Principals try to do too much, too fast." Her suggestions for bringing about effective changes in school culture are simple and practical:

1. Work on team-building.
2. Get acquainted with staff; know where your support is.
3. Focus on doing less rather than more.
4. Facilitate new ideas from groups and individuals.
5. Identify the most important and salient problems.
6. Put your agenda second.
7. Get people excited about the work at hand.
8. Remember that some things just come with time and experience.
9. Learn from students and staff.
10. Accept the fact that it's not all going to get done.
11. Put people before paper.
12. Know that you don't have all the answers; everyone has limitations.
13. Consider the values of staff and students in relation to your own.
14. Ask others' opinions.
15. Get some distance when evaluating changes. (Personal communication, September 13, 1993)

These words of wisdom emphasize the importance of people and relationships. The role of the principal should be to facilitate reforms while at the same time reflecting on how changes affect staff and students. The principal can make a difference only by putting people first.

CONCLUSION

Len Arney, principal of Hamlin Middle School in Springfield, Oregon, observes that "part of the uniqueness and attractiveness of being a principal is that no day is ever the same." Some days are filled with paperwork, meetings with students and staff, and budget concerns. Others are filled with teacher observations, phone calls, and parent conferences. The principals' duties and responsibilities range far and wide.

The challenge for principals, whose busy workdays pull them in a hundred directions at once, is to make each day a positive learning experience for students. An understanding of school culture is an important tool in maintaining this focus on student learning. The lens of culture allows school leaders to shape learning experiences with an eye toward the health of the school community, which inevitably determines the direction and effectiveness of education.

The preceding chapters offer a variety of ways for understanding school culture as well as some suggestions for transforming a culture that does not support excellence into one that does. Recommendations emerge from the literature that guide leaders in rethinking their roles, viewing change systemically, and collaborating with other members of the school community to develop a vision for their schools that exalts excellence while embracing a diversity of thought and opinion.

From their work in a learning consortium, Michael Fullan and Andrew Hargreaves (1991) formulated eight guidelines for how principals should work interactively with teachers and their communities:

1. Understand the culture of the school before trying to change it.

2. Value your teachers: promote their professional growth.
3. Extend what you value.
4. Express what you value.
5. Promote collaboration, not cooptation.
6. Make menus, not mandates.
7. Use bureaucratic means to facilitate, not to constrain.
8. Connect with the wider environment.

These guidelines are not simple solutions, but they do offer some direction to leaders attempting to make changes in school culture.

Still, the most important lesson to be learned by administrators is that they, too, are part of the school culture. A school leader does not make decisions from outside the institution. Change comes as part of the daily routines that affect all participants, including the principal.

Principals who can identify the strengths and weaknesses of their school's culture and see their place in the organization will be more effective school leaders. This simple lesson, remembering one's place in the school organization, can be learned if administrators are willing to approach the process of cultural change with patience, reflection, and humility.

BIBLIOGRAPHY

a'Campo, Charlotte. "Collaborative School Cultures: How Principals Make a Difference." *School Organisation* 13, 2 (1993): 119-27.

Anderson, Carolyn S. "The Search for School Climate: A Review of the Research." *Review of Educational Research* 52, 3 (Fall 1982): 368-420. EJ 273 690.

Arter, Judith A. *Assessing School and Classroom Climate: A Consumer's Guide.* Portland, Oregon: Northwest Regional Educational Laboratory, April 1987. 80 pages. ED 295 301.

Bates, Richard J. "Corporate Culture, Schooling, and Educational Administration." *Educational Administration Quarterly* 23, 4 (1987): 79-115.

Bateson, Gregory. *Steps to an Ecology of Mind.* New York: Ballantine Books, 1972. 541 pages.

Bolman, Lee G., and Terrence E. Deal. "Looking for Leadership: Another Search Party's Report." *Educational Administration Quarterly* 30, 1 (February 1994): 77-96.

Bowers, C. A., and David J. Flinders. *Responsive Teaching. An Ecological Approach to Classroom Patterns of Language, Culture, and Thought.* New York: Teachers College Press, 1990. 271 pages.

Brookover, Wilbur, and others. *School Social Systems and Student Achievement: Schools Can Make a Difference.* New York: Praeger Publishers, 1979. 237 pages.

Burnham, Joan, and Shirley Hord, eds. *Toward Quality in Education: The Leader's Odyssey.* Washington, D.C.: National LEADership Network Study Group on Restructuring Schools, May 1993. 103 pages.

Cavazos, Lauro F., and Christopher T. Cross. "The Principal's Role in Shaping School Culture." *Research in Brief* (March 1990): 1-2.

Cheng, Yin Cheong. "Profiles of Organizational Culture and Effective Schools." *School Effectiveness and School Improvement* 4, 2 (1993): 85-110.

Cunningham, William G., and Donn W. Gresso. *Cultural Leadership: The Culture of Excellence in Education.* Needham Heights, Massachusetts: Allyn & Bacon, 1993. 285 pages.

Deal, Terrence E. "The Culture of Schools." In *Educational Leadership and School Culture,* edited by Marshall Sashkin and Herbert J. Walberg. 3-18. Berkeley, California: McCutchan Publishing, 1993. 182 pages.

_____. "The Culture of Schools." In *Leadership: Examining the Elusive,* edited by Linda T. Scheive and Marion B. Schoenheit. Alexandria, Virginia: Association for Supervision and Curriculum Development, 1987. ED 278 154.

Deal, Terrence E., and Allan A. Kennedy. *Corporate Cultures: The Rites and Rituals of Corporate Life.* Reading, Massachusetts: Addison-Wesley, 1982. 232 pages.

Deal, Terrence E., and Kent D. Peterson. *The Principal's Role in Shaping School Culture.* Washington, D.C.: Office of Educational Research and Improvement, 1990. 122 pages. ED 325 914.

Drake, Thelbert L., and William H. Roe. *The Principalship. 3rd Edition.* New York: Macmillan Publishing Company, 1986. 480 pages.

Endeman, J. "Leadership and Culture: Superintendents and Districts." Paper presented at the American Educational Research Association, Boston, April 20, 1990.

Finlayson, D.S., "School Climate: An Outdated Metaphor?" *Journal of Curriculum Studies* 19, 2 (1987): 163-73.

Firestone, William A., and Bruce L. Wilson. "Bureaucratic and Cultural Linkages: Implications for the Principal." In *Educational Leadership and School Culture,* edited by Marshall Sashkin and Herbert J. Walberg. 19-39. Berkeley, California: McCutchan Publishing, 1993. 182 pages.

Fullan, Michael G. *Change Forces: Probing the Depths of Educational Reform.* Bristo, Pennsylvania: Falmer Press, 1994. 162.

_____. "Visions That Blind." *Educational Leadership* 49, 5 (February 1992): 19-22. EJ 439 278.

Fullan, Michael G., and Andy Hargreaves. *What's Worth Fighting For? Working Together for Your School.* Toronto: Ontario Public School Teachers' Federation, 1991.

Furtwengler, Willis J., and Anita Micich. "Seeing What We Think: Symbols of School Culture." Paper presented at the annual meeting of the American Educational Research Association, Chicago, 1991. 16 pages. ED 335 754.

Fyans, Leslie J., Jr., and Martin L. Maehr. *"School Culture," Student Ethnicity, and Motivation.* Urbana, Illinois: The National Center for School Leadership, 1990. 29 pages. ED 327 947.

Geertz, Clifford. *The Interpretation of Cultures.* New York: Basic Books, 1973. 470 pages.

Glatthorn, Allan A. *Teachers as Agents of Change: A New Look at School Improvement.* Washington, D.C.: National Education Association, 1992. 208 pages. ED 351 787.

Gonder, Peggy Odell, and Donald Hymes. *Improving School Climate and Culture.* Critical Issues Report. Arlington, Virginia: American Association of School Administrators, 1994. 120 pages.

Gottfredson, Denise C., and others. *School Climate Assessment Instruments: A Review.* Baltimore, Maryland: Center for Social Organization of Schools, The John Hopkins University, July 1986. 24 pages. ED 278 702.

Halpin, Andrew W. "The Organizational Climate of Schools." Chapter 4 in *Theory and Research Administration.* 121-249. New York: Macmillan Co., 1966.

Halpin, Andrew W., and Don B. Croft. *The Organizational Climate of Schools.* St. Louis, Missouri: Washington University, 1962. 199 pages.

Hamilton, Mary Lynn, and Virginia Richardson. "Effects of the Culture in Two Schools on the Process and Outcomes of Staff Development." *The Elementary School Journal* 95, 4 (March 1995): 367-380.

Harvey, Michael J. "Strategy for the New Principal: Negotiating the Culture of the School." Paper presented at the Australian Council for Educational Administration, Sea World Nara Resort, Gold Coast, September 1991. ED 359 670.

Heckman, Paul E. "School Restructuring in Practice: Reckoning with the Culture of School." *International Journal of Educational Reform* 2, 3 (July 1993): 263-71.

Hickman, Craig R., and Michael A. Silva. *Creating Excellence: Managing Corporate Culture, Strategy, and Change in the New Age.* New York: New American Library, 1984. 305 pages.

Howard, Eugene R., and James W. Keefe. *The CASE-IMS School Improvement Process: Suggested Components of a School Design Statement.* (January 1994). Working Draft for the NASSP School Design Project.

_____. *The CASE-IMS School Improvement Process.* Reston, Virginia: National Association of Secondary School Principals,

1991. 44 pages. ED 342 089.

Hoy, Wayne K., and Sharon I. R. Clover. "Elementary School Climate: A Revision of the OCDQ." *Educational Administration Quarterly* 22, 1 (Winter 1986): 93-110. EJ 337 441.

Keefe, James W. "Leadership for School Restructuring—Redesigning Your School." *High School Magazine* 1, 2 (December 1993): 4-9.

Keefe, James W., and Edgar A. Kelley. "Comprehensive Assessment and School Improvement." *NASSP Bulletin* 74, 530 (December 1990): 54-63. EJ 418 214.

Keefe, James W., and others. "A Comprehensive System for School Planning and Improvement." In *Advances in Educational Productivity*, Vol. 3, edited by Herbert Walberg. 257-84. Greenwich, Connecticut: JAI Press, 1993.

Kowalski, Theodore, J. *Planning and Managing School Facilities.* New York: Praeger, 1989. 215 pages.

Kozol, Jonathan. *Savage Inequalities: Children in American Schools.* New York: Crown Publishers, 1991. 262 pages. ED 356 035.

Krug, Samuel E. *Instructional Leadership, School Instructional Climate, and Student Learning Outcomes.* Washington, D.C.: United States Department of Education; and Urbana, Illionois: National Center for School Leadership, June 1992. 26 pages.

Lane, Bruce A. "Cultural Leaders in Effective Schools: The Builders and Brokers of Excellence." *NASSP Bulletin* (February 1992): 85-96.

Leithwood, Kenneth, and Doris Jantzi. "Transformational Leadership: How Principals Can Help Reform School Cultures." Paper presented at the annual meeting of the American Educational Research Association, Boston, April 16-20, 1990. 49 pages. ED 323 622.

Leithwood, Kenneth; Doris Jantzi; and Alicia Fernandez. "Transformational Leadership and Teachers' Commitment to Changes." In *Reshaping the Principalship, Insights from Transformational Reform Efforts,* edited by Joseph Murphy and Karen Seashore Louis. 77-98. Thousand Oaks, California: Corwin Press, 1994.

Liontos, Lynn Balster. *Transformational Leadership. Profile of a High School Principal.* OSSC Bulletin Series. Eugene: Oregon School Study Council, University of Oregon, July 1993. 57 pages. ED 359 652.

Louis, Karen Seashore; Helen M. Marks; and Sharon Kruse. "Teachers' Professional Community in Restructuring Schools." Madison, Wisconsin: Center on Organization and Restructuring of Schools, December 6, 1994. 58 pages.

Maehr, Martin L. "The 'Psychological Environment' of the School: A Focus for School Leadership." Project Report. Urbana, Illinois: National Center for School Leadership, 1990. 69 pages. ED 327 954.

_____. "Transforming School Culture to Enhance Motivation." Paper presented at annual meeting of American Education Research Association, San Francisco, April 20-24, 1992. 20 pages. ED 350 668.

Maehr, Martin, and Rachel Buck. "Transforming School Culture." In *Educational Leadership and School Culture*, edited by Marshall Sashkin and Herbert J. Walberg. 40-60. Berkeley, California: McCutchan Publishing, 1993. 182 pages.

Maehr, Martin, and Leslie J. Fyans, Jr. "School Culture, Motivation and Achievement." In *Advances in Motivation and Achievement, Vol 6: Motivation Enhancing Environments*, edited by Martin L. Maehr and Carole Ames. 215-47. Greenwich, Connecticut: JAI Press, 1989.

Maehr, Martin L., and Stephanie A. Parker. "A Tale of Two Schools—and the Primary Task of Leadership." *Phi Delta Kappan* (November 1993): 233-39.

Martel, Laurence D., "Building a Learning Community." *School Administrator* 50, 6 (June 1993): 22-27. EJ 465 274.

Maxwell, T.W., and A. Ross Thomas. "School Climate and School Culture." *Journal of Educational Administration* 29, 2 (1991): 72-82. EJ 525 826.

Peters, Thomas J., and Robert H. Waterman, Jr. *In Search of Excellence: Lessons from America's Best-Run Companies*. New York: Harper and Row, 1982. 360 pages.

Pierson, Patricia R., and Paul V. Bredeson. "It's Not Just a Laughing Matter: School Principals' Use of Humor in Interpersonal Communications with Teachers." *Journal of School Leadership* 3, 5 (September 1993): 522-33. EJ 466 909.

Renchler, Ron. *Student Motivation, School Culture, and Academic Achievement: What School Leaders Can Do*. Trends and Issues Series. Eugene, Oregon: ERIC Clearinghouse on Educational Management., University of Oregon, February 1992. 26 pages. ED 351 741.

Rutter, Michael, and others. *Fifteen Thousand Hours: Secondary Schools and Their Effects on Childern*. Cambridge, Massachusetts: Harvard University Press, 1979. 285 pages.

Sashkin, Marshall. "The Visionary Principal: School Leadership for the Next Century." In *Educational Leadership and School Culture,* edited by Marshall Sashkin and Herbert J. Walberg. 75-88. Berkeley, California: McCutchan Publishing, 1993. 182 pages.

Sashkin, Marshall, and others. "Assessing Transformational Leadership and Its Impact." In *Impact of Leadership*, edited by Kenneth E. Clark, Miriam B. Clark, and David P. Campbell. 131-48. Greensboro, North Carolina: Center for Creative Leadership, 1992.

Sashkin, Marshall, and Sashkin, Molly G. "Leadership and Culture Building in Schools: Quantitative and Qualitative Understandings." Paper presented at the annual meeting of the American Educational Research Association, Boston, April 16-20, 1990. 41 pages. ED 322 583.

Schein, Edgar H. "Coming to a New Awareness of Corporate Culture." *Sloan Management Review* 25 (1984): 3-16.

_____. *Organizational Culture and Leadership.* San Francisco: Jossey-Bass, 1985. 358 pages.

Schwartz, Audrey James. "School Social Context, Teacher Culture, and School-Based Management." Paper presented at the annual meeting of the American Educational Research Association, Boston, April 16-20, 1990. 20 pages. EA 022 064.

Senge, Peter M. "The Leader's New Work: Building Learning Organizations." *Sloan Management Review* (Fall 1990): 7-23.

Sergiovanni, Thomas J. *The Principalship: A Reflective Practice Perspective.* Newton, Massachusetts: Allyn and Bacon, 1987. ED 283 275.

Sheffield, Anne, and Bruce Frankel, eds. *When I Was Young I Loved School: Dropping Out and Hanging In.* New York: Children's Express Foundation, 1989. 213 pages.

Steele, Fritz, and Stephen Jenks. *The Feel of the Work Place: Understanding and Improving Organization Climate.* Reading, Massachusetts: Addison-Wesley, 1977. 194 pages.

Thacker, Jerry L., and William D. McInerney. "Changing Academic Culture to Improve Student Achievement in the Elementary Schools." *ERS Spectrum* 10, 4 (Fall 1992): 18-23. EJ 454 390.

Witcher, Ann E. "Assessing School Climate: An Important Step for Enhancing School Quality." *NASSP Bulletin* 77, 554 (September 1993): 1-5.

COMMENTS ON THIS BOOK

*by Selected Scholars
and Leaders in Education*

Before this book went to press, the Clearing-house followed its usual procedure of inviting experts in the field to contribute endorsements of the book for quotation on the back cover. A cover letter signed by the Clearinghouse's director, Philip K. Piele, and proof copies were sent to several professors of educational administration, leaders of professional organizations of teachers and administrators, and others who have established reputations for their work on school culture.

The comments we received went way beyond what could fit on the back cover. Because the remarks were so thoughtful and helpful in understanding both the subject of school culture and how the content of this book relates to other literature on the topic, we decided to include here, in alphabetical order, the full text of each respondent's comment.

Roland Barth
Founding Director, Harvard Principals' Center

School culture is a soft concept with very hard effects upon educators and those they would educate. All too many school cultures are toxic, inhospitable to the development of both community and of learning—let alone of a community of learners. Regrettably, the culture of an organization subtly but surely influences its inhabitants far more than they deliberately shape it.

Principals will find in this tidy little volume considerable clarity about the fuzzy concept of school culture. They will respond to the rich examples from practice which help to detect the important elements of a school's culture. And they will find immensely valuable and useful the suggestions offered, which will aid them in actively influencing their school's culture to bring it into closer alignment with a desired vision.

What an ambitious—and very successful—lesson plan!

Edwin M. Bridges
Professor of Education, Stanford University

Transforming School Culture offers valuable guidance to principals on how to build a school vision and how to effect meaningful changes in their school culture.

Keith Geiger
President, National Education Association

Stephen Stolp and Stuart Smith remind us that, for better or worse, each school has a unique culture and "climate." Successful administrators and teachers are not casual about the kind of culture that takes root in their school. Instead, they take an active, catalytic role in shaping a school culture that values children and places a premium on high expectations. The authors make a superb case that school leaders must tap the full potential of rituals, ceremonies, and traditions in transforming their school's culture.

William D. Greenfield, Jr.
Professor of Education, Portland State University

I think that *Transforming School Culture: Stories, Symbols, Values, and the Leader's Role* will make a fine contribution to the literature informing the improvement of school practices. It is highly readable and I think that school principals and other leaders at the school site will find it a useful guide to efforts to shape, sustain, and/or change their school climate and culture.

One of the things that is missing in a lot of the discussions and reports about school culture is concrete guidance about how teachers and school administrators can influence the culture of their school. This book nicely fills that void.

It offers a straight-forward approach to understanding a very complex idea, and the suggestions discussed in the book are amply illustrated with good examples.

Principals and teacher leaders interested in influencing the important connections between school culture and school reform efforts will find this book valuable. Descriptions about the differences between school culture and various other aspects of the school organization, like communication and decision-making patterns, levels of commitment to change, and the effects of school leadership, offer readers a rich array of key variables, relationships, and strategies associated with school culture and change.

Paul Houston
Executive Director, American Association of School Administrators

Stolp and Smith, in their new book, *Transforming School Culture: Stories, Symbols, Values, and the Leaders' Role,* capture the elusive, but powerful source of what spells the difference between success and failure for today's leader. They expound and enhance the true *spirit* of the organization. In doing so, they add a strong new view of leadership in today's chaotic world.

James W. Keefe
Director of Research, National Association of Secondary School Principals

Culture is the response of human beings to their environments. Different environments evoke different cultures.

School leaders, teachers, and community members will better understand what complex systems schools really are and why school change can be so challenging after reading *Transforming School Culture—Stories, Symbols, Values, and the Leader's Role.* Stephen Stolp and Stuart Smith explore a variety of ways to understand and to transform school culture and climate in this readable book. In particular, they clarify the key relationships between the two concepts and leaders' new roles in supporting school learning communities.

Anyone interested in knowing why past efforts at school

restructuring have tended to fail, and why cultural transformation must precede structural change in schools, should read this volume very carefully.

Samual G. Sava
Executive Director, National Association of Elementary School Principals

A school's "culture" or "spirit" are surely among the most difficult education terms to define. Instead of approaching the task in a dry academic manner, giving us yet another formulation to forget, Stolp and Smith explain by example, giving us people and incidents to illustrate that every school has a distinctive culture; the only question is, Does the culture aid schooling or impede it?

Most important, the authors show how principals and teachers can shape the school's culture to their own purposes, rather than becoming its passive victims.

This is a refreshing contribution to our professional literature.

Albert Shanker
President, American Federation of Teachers

Anyone who's ever worked in a school will recognize the power of what the authors call *school culture*. This book provides practical guidance to school leaders who want to understand school culture and use it as a lever of change. Stolp and Smith have their focus right, on the need for collaboration among school staff, the importance of data, and improved student learning as the ultimate goal of cultural change.

OTHER TITLES

Children at the Center: Implementing the Multiage Classroom
Bruce A. Miller • 1994 • 8 1/2 x 11 inches • xii + 123 pages • perfect (sew/wrap) bind • ISBN: 0-86552-130-1 • $15.95 **Code: EMOCAC**

"Changing to a multiage classroom reflects a magnitude of change far greater than simply changing to a new textbook or learning a new strategy or program," notes Bruce Miller, researcher at the Northwest Regional Educational Laboratory. "Implementing multiage instruction and organization represents a major shift in classroom norms."

In this richly descriptive book, Miller examines multiage programs at four elementary schools. Developed by the Laboratory and the Clearinghouse, the book shares firsthand insights of teachers and administrators who made the change from graded to multiage classrooms. In addition, it draws upon survey responses from participants in a national multiage conference and offers guidelines for a smooth transition to a multiage structure.

Although Miller stresses that there is no single model or recipe for becoming a multiage classroom or school, he identifies a number of incremental steps that can facilitate change and improve the likelihood of success.

Planning for Effective Staff Development: Six Research-Based Models
Meredith D. "Mark" Gall, Roseanne O'Brien Vojtek • 1994 • x + 54 pages • 6 x 9 • saddle bind • ISBN: 0-86552-126-3 • $6.95. **Code: EMOPFE**

This brief monograph organizes staff development objectives, models, and program-design features into an understandable, comprehensive framework.

In part 1, Gall and O'Brien Vojtek advise readers to weigh each program's objectives. They discuss eight main types of objectives—five teacher-centered objectives, a student-centered objective, a curriculum-centered objective, and a school-centered objective.

Part 2 features six major models of staff development. Each model represents a different strategy for accomplishing one or more of the objectives identified in part 1. The models are summarized, their key features noted, and the objectives for which they are best suited are listed.

Specific program characteristics or features that influence the effectiveness of various staff development objectives receive attention in part 3. Nineteen features are grouped under three categories: objectives, delivery system, and administration.

Implementing Problem-Based Learning in Leadership Development

Edwin M. Bridges and Philip Hallinger • 1995 • xii + 194 pages☐ • perfect (sew/wrap) bind • ISBN 0-86552-131-X • $14.95. **Code: EMOIPB**

Problem-based learning (PBL) is a concept borrowed from the medical field. It is a training strategy in which students, working in groups, take responsibility for solving professional problems. The instructor creates a hypothetical situation for the students (called a *project*) and then takes a back seat as an observer and an advisor while the students work out a solution. Pertinent problems can be the hiring of a new teacher, the creation of an AIDS education program, or the construction of a school improvement plan.

This book builds on the authors' experiences in using PBL in a variety of settings. They discuss the operation of PBL in the classroom and describe their template for developing PBL instructional materials. In examining the role of the instructor, the authors highlight the attitudes, thinking, and behaviors essential to successful implementation of PBL. They also address evaluation of student performance, and illustrate options for incorporating PBL into Ed.D. research projects.

Managing the Incompetent Teacher

Edwin M. Bridges with the assistance of Barry☐ Groves • Second Edition • 1990 • 84 pages • saddle bind • ISBN 0-86552-102-6 • $7.95. **Code: EMOMIC**

Bridges presents an integrated organizational approach in which teacher dismissal becomes a logical extension of overall school policy. "Superintendents who follow this systematic approach should be able to upgrade the quality of their teaching staff, to increase the incidence of dismissal when teachers fail to improve, and to heighten the prospects of winning a dismissal case if it is contested by the teacher."

The Collaborative School: A Work Environment for Effective Instruction

Stuart C. Smith and James J. Scott • Foreword by Roland S. Barth • 1990 • xii + 77 pages • perfect bind • ISBN 0-86552-092-5 • $9.00. **Code: EMOTSC**

What are *collaborative schools*? In contrast to many schools where the adults work in isolation from one another, teachers and administrators in collaborative schools work as a team. Through such practices as mutual help, exchange of ideas, joint planning, and participation in decisions, the faculty and administrators improve their own skills and the effectiveness of their schools.

This book outlines the educational benefits of collaboration, describes a variety of collaborative practices already in use in schools, and suggests ideas for introducing those practices in other schools that wish to become more collaborative.

Roadmap to Restructuring: Policies, Practices, and the Emerging Visions of Schooling

David T. Conley • 1993 • 6 x 9 inches • xvi + 432 pages • Perfect (sew/wrap) bind • ISBN 0-86552-120-4 • $19.95. **Code: EMORSC**

By weaving together more than 600 sources as well as his own experience as a consultant to restructuring schools, David T. Conley, an associate professor at the University of Oregon, offers a clear sense of the "lay of the land" of restructuring.

The term *restructuring* "is as notable for its ambiguity as for its meaning," Conley states. He begins by distinguishing it from two other terms that are used to describe educational change—*reform* and *renewal*. His own definition ties restructuring to improved student learning.

Twenty-six chapters are divided into four parts. After clarifying various approaches to change in the introduction, Conley fixes the current restructuring movement in a context in part 1. In part 2, Conley zeros in on the relationship between central office and school, the role of teachers, and the community's link to education.

In part 3, the centerpiece of the book, Conley sets forth a framework of twelve dimensions of restructuring. These dimensions have been constructed to assist educators in sorting out the plethora of projects taking place under the banner of restructuring. Part 4, "Process of Restructuring," tackles issues relevant to implementation.

Directory of Organizations in Educational Management

Ninth Edition☐ • Stuart C. Smith and Meta S. Bruner, compilers
• 1994 • 70 pages • saddle bind • ISSN 0070-6035 • $8.50. **Code: EDIR94**

The most comprehensive resource of its kind, this Directory provides access to organizations that are sources of information on educational management at the elementary and secondary levels.

Listed in this edition are a total of 163 organizations that are engaged in research and development or that provide services to the profession, such as consultation, information, exchange of ideas, or workshops. The listings give each agency's address, phone and fax numbers, chief executive officer, purpose, subject areas, topics of available publications, periodicals, and services.

VALUE SEARCHES

Value Searches are economical, user friendly collections of ERIC resumés on high-demand topics.

The resumés (bibliographic data and abstracts) are printed in large type, and they are durably bound. Whereas an original ERIC database search would cost a minimum of $30.00, Value Searches are priced at only $7.50 each. Each Value Search is updated periodically.

- Multiage or Nongraded Education **Code: EVSMNE**
- Total Quality Management **Code: EVSTQM**
- Class Size **Code: EVSCLS**
- School Restructuring **Code: EVSSDR**
- School Choice, Vouchers, Charter Schools, and Open Enrollment **Code: EVSSCC**
- Parent Involvement in the Educational Process **Code: EVSPIV**
- Instructional Leadership **Code: EVSILO**
- Leadership of Effective Schools **Code: EVSLES**
- Collegiality, Participative Decision-Making and the☐ Collaborative Scho☐ode: EVSCPD
- At-Risk Youth and Dropout Prevention **Code: EVSARD**

Full payment or purchase order must accompany all orders. A $3.00 shipping/handling fee is added to all orders. Make checks payable to **University of Oregon/ERIC.** Allow 6-8 weeks for delivery. (To expedite delivery, you may request UPS for an additional charge.) **The ERIC/CEM unconditional guarantee:** You must be completely satisfied with every book you purchase or return it to us within 60 days for a full refund or credit.

ERIC CLEARINGHOUSE ON EDUCATIONAL MANAGEMENT

5207 University of Oregon, Eugene, Oregon 97403-5207.

800-438-8841

"Principals will respond to the rich examples from practice which help to detect the important elements of a school's culture."

Roland Barth, Founding Director, Harvard Principals' Center

"Offers valuable guidance to principals on how to build a school vision and how to effect meaningful changes in their school culture."

Edwin M. Bridges, Professor of Education, Stanford University

"The authors make a superb case that school leaders must tap the full potential of rituals, ceremonies, and traditions in transforming their school's culture."

Keith Geiger, President, NEA

"One of the things that is missing in a lot of the discussions and reports about school culture is concrete guidance about how teachers and school administrators can influence the culture of their school. This book nicely fills that void."

William D. Greenfield, Jr., Professor of Education, Portland State University

"Stolp and Smith . . . capture the elusive, but powerful source of what spells the difference between success and failure for today's leader."

Paul Houston, Executive Director, AASA

"Anyone interested in knowing why past efforts at school restructuring have tended to fail, and why cultural transformation must precede structural change in schools, should read this volume very carefully."

James W. Keefe, Director of Research, NASSP

"The authors show how principals and teachers can shape the school's culture to their own purposes, rather than becoming its passive victims."

Samual G. Sava, Executive Director, NAESP

"Stolp and Smith have their focus right, on the need for collaboration among school staff, the importance of data, and improved student learning as the ultimate goal of cultural change."

Albert Shanker, President, AFT

*   *   *

For the complete comments from which the above quotes were taken, see pages 89-92.

CLEARINGHOUSE
ON EDUCATIONAL MANAGEMENT
UNIVERSITY OF OREGON

Printed in the United States
821300004B